Twayne's English Authors Series

Sylvia E. Bowman, *Editor*

INDIANA UNIVERSITY

Bernard Mandeville

 170

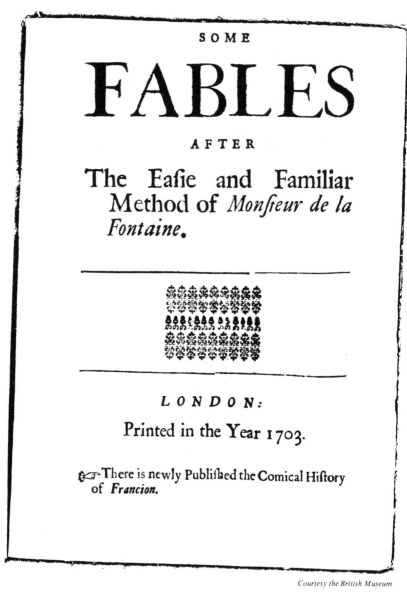

A photo facsimile of the Title Page of Bernard Mandeville's first publication in English

Bernard Mandeville

By RICHARD I. COOK

Kent State University

Twayne Publishers, Inc.   : :   New York

Library of Congress Cataloging in Publication Data

Cook, Richard I
  Bernard Mandeville.

  (Twayne's English authors series, TEAS 170)
  Bibliography: p. 165.
  1. Mandeville, Bernard, 1670-1733—Criticism and
interpretation.
PR3545.M6Z6   192   73-21513
ISBN 0-8057-1371-9

PR
3545
,M6
Z6

66882

Preface

Although Bernard Mandeville is the author of a considerable and varied body of work, his present reputation has come to rest almost exclusively upon *The Fable of the Bees*. Clearly, the immense literary vitality of *The Fable*, augmented by its importance in the histories of economic and moral philosophy, more than justifies its preeminence, though one may regret that among the effects of that preeminence has been the near eclipse of Mandeville's subsidiary works. In recent years, a number of Mandeville's minor writings have been reissued in facsimile editions; but, for the most part, his lesser works have remained little known and, indeed, unobtainable, except in libraries with extensive rare-book collections. Mandeville's writings as a whole have never been the subject of a book-length study, and one of the purposes of this volume is to offer those who know Mandeville only through his masterpiece a general introduction to the full range of his work. Accordingly, I have sought to survey, with particular emphasis upon the less familiar writings, all those works (except for a few brief journalistic and medical pieces) which can be confidently attributed to Mandeville.

Since the scope of this series is limited and since my major concern is with the writings themselves, I have not treated at length the extensive literature of controversy inspired by Mandeville's works. Nor have I, except in passing, dealt with such nonliterary matters as the current disagreement between economic historians concerning Mandeville's precise relationship to the doctrines of *laissez-faire*. Readers who are interested in pursuing these topics, however, will find relevant materials listed in the selected bibliography at the end of the volume.

In the preface to his *Free Thoughts on Religion, the Church, and National Happiness* Mandeville, after announcing his great indebtedness to Pierre Bayle, goes on to explain that the very size of the debt has made detailed acknowledgments unfeasible, since *"I imagin'd, that it would be unpleasant, if not disgustful, to see the same Name so often repeated in the Notes...."* For much the same reasons, I have not in every instance documented my own debt to F. B. Kaye, whose splendid edition of *The Fable of the Bees* and whose work in establishing the Mandeville canon furnish the starting points for any study of Mandeville. If I have not always agreed with Kaye's specific interpretations, I have nevertheless found him (as have all modern students of Mandeville) an indispensable source of illuminating ideas and fundamental information.

RICHARD I. COOK

Kent State University

Contents

Chronology

1670   Bernard Mandeville baptized November 20, in Rotterdam.

1685   Mandeville completes his final year at the Erasmian School in Rotterdam. In October, matriculates at the University of Leyden; publishes the required oration, *De Medicina Oratio Scholastica.*

1689   March 23, presents his dissertation in philosophy at Leyden—*Disputatio Philosophica de Brutorum Operationibus.*

1691   March 30, Mandeville receives his Doctor of Medicine degree at Leyden—dissertation entitled *Disputatio Medica Inauguralis de Chylosi Vitiata.*

1692?   Visits England to learn the language; decides to move there.

1699   February 1. Now resident in England, Mandeville marries Ruth Elizabeth Laurence.

1703   Publishes his first work in English—*Some Fables After the Easie and Familiar Manner of Monsieur de la Fontaine.*

1704   *Some Fables* reissued, with new material, as *Aesop Dress'd: Or, a Collection of Fables Writ in Familiar Verse.*

1704   Publishes *Typhon: Or, the Wars Between the Gods and Giants: A Burlesque Poem in Imitation of the Comical Mons. Scarron.*

1705   Publishes *The Grumbling Hive: Or, Knaves Turn'd Honest.*

1709   Publishes *The Virgin Unmask'd: Or, Female Dialogues Betwixt an Elderly Maiden Lady, and Her Niece.*

1711   Publishes *A Treatise of the Hypochondriack and Hysterick Passions.*

1712   Publishes *Wishes to a Godson, With Other Miscellany Poems.*

1714   *The Fable of the Bees: Or, Private Vices, Publick Benefits* appears. In addition to the original *Grumbling Hive*, this work contains twenty prose "Remarks" on the text and "An Enquiry into the Origins of Moral Virtue."

1720   Publishes *Free Thoughts on Religion, the Church, and National Happiness.*

1723   *The Fable of the Bees* is reprinted, with the "Remarks" expanded and two new essays included—"A Search Into the Nature of Society" and "An Essay on Charity and Charity-Schools." For the first time, *The Fable* attracts public attention.

1724   Publishes *A Modest Defence of Publick Stews. The Fable of the Bees* is presented by the Grand Jury of Middlesex County; Mandeville reissues *The Fable,* enlarging the preface and adding "A Vindication of the Book, From the Aspersions Contain'd in a Presentment of the Grand Jury of Middlesex, and an Abusive Letter to Lord C."

1725   Publishes *An Enquiry into the Causes of the Frequent Executions at Tyburn.*

1728   Publishes *The Fable of the Bees,* Part II (title page dated 1729).

1732   Publishes *An Enquiry into the Origin of Honour, and the Usefulness of Christianity in War.* Mandeville's final work—*A Letter to Dion, Occasion'd by His Book Call'd Alciphron*—appears.

1733   January 21, Mandeville dies at Hackney.

CHAPTER 1

Life of Mandeville

TO attempt a sketch of the life of Bernard Mandeville is to be confronted at once by a simple scarcity of knowledge, for such biographical information as we have consists mostly of a handful of bare facts gleaned from public records. From church registries, university archives, and other such documentary sources, we may learn many of the important dates in Mandeville's life; but this sort of information can give us little more than the skeletal structure of a man's career. The materials which might flesh out a portrait—private letters, diaries, reminiscences of friends—are in Mandeville's case very few. Even so assiduous an investigator as F. B. Kaye could discover little in the way of reliable primary sources to augment the vital statistics of Mandeville's life.[1]

Naturally, as a controversialist in matters of ethics and religion, Mandeville did not lack for commentators; but their impressions of his character and personality (as we shall see) are usually secondhand and are almost always strongly colored by righteous indignation over the presumed scandalous import of his philosophy. The satanic Mandeville portrayed by his enemies bears little resemblance to the genial explicator of awkward truths who emerges from the works themselves. Behind both of these public personalities, we may assume, lurked a more private Mandeville, but that Mandeville remains a shadowy figure.

Bernard de Mandeville (after 1715 he dropped the particle in his name) was born in 1670 in or near Rotterdam, where on November 20 of that year he was baptized in the Reformed Church. The family name, which suggests a French ancestry, first appears in Holland at Nijmegen, the city in which the author's great-grandfather Michael (d. 1635) was a prominent physician, as well as an alderman and the rector of the Latin

School. Michael's son, Emmanuel (1611–1660), likewise practiced medicine, as did the author's father, Michael de Mandeville (b. 1639). With so distinguished a family tradition of
medicine, it was only natural that the young Bernard, while
attending Rotterdam's Erasmian School, should choose a medical subject for his required scholastic oration. *De Medicina
Oratio Scholastica,* Mandeville's first extant work, was published at Rotterdam in 1685, and in October of that year he
matriculated at the University of Leyden with the declared
intention of becoming a physician.

Despite his medical interests, Mandeville's initial registry
at Leyden was as a student of philosophy; and his dissertation,
submitted in 1689, was titled *Disputatio Philosophica de
Brutorum Operationibus,* wherein he argued the Cartesian
case for automatism in animals. Some two years later, however,
Mandeville had completed his medical training; and in March,
1691, he received his degree as Doctor of Medicine. In *A
Treatise of the Hypochondriack and Hysterick Passions* (1711),
one of the few works in which he offers autobiographical information, Mandeville recalls the occasion. Philopirio, the physician whom Mandeville admits is intended to represent the
author, tells Misomedon, his patient:

It is the custom in all our Foreign Universities for Students in all
Faculties, after having pass'd the several Examinations they are to
undergo, before they take their Degree, to compose and defend
against all that will oppose a *Thesis* or Disputation, the Theme of
which is what they are pleas'd to chuse themselves, and always some
Head or Point relating to the Profession they belong to. . . .

Mine was [*Disputatio Medica Inauguralis*] *de Chylosi Vitiata,*
which I defended at *Leyden* in the Year 1691, Dr. *William Senguerdus,*
Professor of the *Aristotelian* Philosophy, being then *Rector Mag-
nificus.* My reason of telling you this, which otherwise might seem
impertinent, is because I have often thought it very remarkable, that
I always had a particular Eye upon, and have been led, as it were,
by instinct to what afterwards to me appear'd to be the cause of
the Hysterick and Hypochondriack Passions, even at a time, when
I had no thought of singling out these Distempers for my more particular Study, and was only design'd for general Practice, as other
Physicians are.[2]

As this passage suggests, Mandeville's original intention of
serving a general practice soon gave way to his growing convic-

tion that "every Physician, that would discharge his Conscience, ought as much, as he can in his private Capacity, to . . . apply himself to the study of one Distemper only."[3] Accordingly, he began to concentrate his studies upon nervous disorders—a choice which was at least in part dictated by the fact that his father had specialized in the same field. "I should hardly have ventur'd upon [this study]," Philopirio tells Misemedon, "if I had not seen something of it, *a teneris,* and been led into it by the long experience of a Father before me, who, when he died had been a Physician above 38 Years, in two very Populous Cities. . . ."[4]

I *Travels to England and Marriage*

It is not certain for how long, if indeed at all, Mandeville practiced medicine in Holland. The evidence suggests that at least some of his time after completion of his studies may have been spent in travel through France and Italy. At some time in the early or mid-1690's, Mandeville journeyed to London, his purpose being, as he later explained, "to learn the Language; in which having happen'd to take great delight, and in the mean time found the Country and the Manners of it agreeable to his Humour, he has now been many Years, and is like to end his days in *England*."[5] Having made his choice, Mandeville embraced his new nationality with a steady, if sometimes critical, sense of patriotism.

In *The Fable of the Bees* and his other works he writes on the assumption, which he shares with his readers, that England, whatever her faults, culturally, religiously, politically, and commercially represents the best in European civilization. Except for the few explicitly autobiographical passages in *A Treatise of the Hypochondriack and Hysterick Passions,* Mandeville's published works in English make no specific reference to his Dutch origins, though he frequently cites Holland by way of both good and bad example in matters of government and custom. Typical of his comments are the remarks on Holland in *The Virgin Unmask'd* (1709). As England's principal ally against France in the War of the League of Augsburg (1689–1697) and the War of the Spanish Succession (1702–1713), the Dutch had been much criticized in England by the Tory opposition for allegedly failing to contribute their proportionate share to the war effort. Against such charges Mandeville offers a vigorous defense, only to balance it a few pages later by some disparaging remarks on the way that "the *Dutch* Boors, valuing themselves upon what they save by being penurious, have a Hatred and Aversion against every Thing that seems more civiliz'd than themselves."[6]

By February 1, 1698, Mandeville had sufficiently established himself in London to take a wife; and he married on that date Ruth Elizabeth Laurence at St. Giles-in-the-Fields. Of his wife (referred to as Elizabeth in his will) almost nothing is known, but the church records give her age at the time of marriage as twenty-five. She was to bear him at least two children—a son, Michael, and a daughter, Penelope.

II *Publications*

In the opinion of Lucinda, the elderly maiden lady who in *The Virgin Unmask'd* so learnedly discourses to her young niece on the ways of the world, "there is not one in ten thousand that ever attains to that Perfection in another Language, as to understand the Beauties of it, as well as he does those of his own."[7] By 1709 Mandeville could record these words with some complacency, for he had already more than demonstrated his mastery of English as early as 1703 when he published his first work in his adopted language. In *Some Fables After the Easie and Familiar Method of Monsieur de la Fontaine*, Mandeville made his debut as an English author with twenty-nine fables in verse, two of his own invention and the rest adapted from La Fontaine. *Some Fables* was published anonymously, though by 1704, when Mandeville issued his second English volume, *Typhon: Or the Wars Between the Gods and Giants: A Burlesque Poem in Imitation of the Comical Mons. Scarron*, he went so far as to attach his initials to the Epistle Dedicatory.[8] It was also in 1704 that Mandeville reissued the earlier work, this time under the title *Aesop Dress'd: Or, a Collection of Fables Writ in Familiar Verse*, adding ten new fables and allowing his name to appear on the title page. One year later, in 1705, Mandeville's career as a verse fabulist was capped by the publication of *The Grumbling Hive: Or, Knaves Turn'd Honest*, the nucleus around which over the next twenty-four years he would develop his major work, *The Fable of the Bees*.

In *The Virgin Unmask'd: Or, Female Dialogues Betwixt an Elderly Maiden Lady, and Her Niece, on Several Diverting Discourses on Love, Marriage, Memoirs, and Morals &c of the Times* (1709), Mandeville produced his first volume of English prose. The dialogue proved a particularly congenial form to Mandeville, for it provided him with a perfect format for his conversational prose style and for the wide-ranging social and philosophical commentary which was his major concern. Though he produced in 1712 another volume of poetry, *Wishes to a Godson, With Other Miscellany Poems*, he turned to prose and, often as not, to the dialogue, in all his subsequent books. In this form he chose to cast his sole medical work in English, the book which in its full descriptive title appeared as *A Treatise of the Hypochondriack and Hysterick Passions, Vulgarly call'd the Hypo in Men and Vapours in Women; In which the Symptoms, Causes, and Cure of those Diseases are set forth after a Method intirely new. The whole interspers'd, with Instructive Discourses on the Real Art of Physick it self; and Entertaining Remarks on the Modern Practice of Physicians and Apothecaries: Very useful to all, that have the Misfortune to stand in need of either* (1711).

In 1714, Mandeville reissued *The Grumbling Hive*, his verse fable of nine years before, but on this occasion he added an extensive prose commentary consisting of *An Enquiry into the Origin of Moral Virtue* and some twenty "Remarks" elaborating upon the ideas expressed in the poem. The new volume was called *The Fable of the Bees: Or, Private Vices, Publick Benefits*, an elliptical subtitle whose ambiguity later helped Mandeville earn his reputation as a subverter of public morality. By 1720, when Mandeville issued his *Free Thoughts on Religion, the Church, and National Happiness*, he had published some nine volumes in English, and neither singly nor collectively had they brought him more than a very modest share of the fame that he candidly admits he hoped to achieve by his writings.[9]

That fame, in the form of notoriety, was to come to Mandeville in 1723 with the publication of a new and enlarged edition of *The Fable of the Bees*. To the 1714 version Mandeville added two lengthy essays—"A Search into the Nature of Society" and "An Essay on Charity and Charity-Schools"—and he also enlarged the explanatory "Remarks."

The response (which will be discussed later) was immediate, for the 1723 *Fable of the Bees* attracted voluminous, if mostly hostile, attention. It was widely reviewed and denounced, both in print and from the pulpit.[10] The book was twice presented by the Grand Jury of Middlesex as a public nuisance. Overnight Mandeville had, as Kaye puts it, "inherited the office of Lord High Bogy-man, which Hobbes had held in the preceding century."[11]

Judging from his publications during the ten years that remained to him, Mandeville seems to have rather enjoyed his new role as a public gadfly. Though he defended himself with vigor and good humor against those who claimed he was an advocate of vice, certain of his ensuing works were of a nature clearly more apt to increase than to pacify the outrage that had been elicited by the *Fable*. In 1724, Mandeville, developing an idea he had already briefly expressed in "Remark H" of the *Fable*, published a pamphlet entitled *A Modest Defence of Publick Stews: Or, An Essay upon Whoring, as it is now practis'd in these Kingdoms*, wherein he proposes the establishment of a series of government brothels to be licensed and administered by Parliament. In this same year he also published a new edition of the *Fable* which contained the Grand Jury's presentment against the 1723 edition, an "abusive Letter to Lord *C*" concerning the *Fable* (reprinted from the *London Journal* of July 27, 1723), and his own "Vindication" of the book. Mandeville appeared once more as a projector in 1725 with *An Enquiry into the Causes of the Frequent Executions at Tyburn: And a Proposal for some Regulations concerning Felons in Prison, and the good Effects to be Expected from them. To which is Added, a Discourse on Transportation, and a Method to render that Punishment more Effectual*.

Meanwhile, the attacks upon the *Fable* continued to multiply; and in 1729 Mandeville doubled its size (completing the work as we have it now) by adding six dialogues in which Cleomenes, a Mandevillian, triumphantly demonstrates to Horatio the inadequacy of Shaftesburian optimism. The final works from Mandeville's pen—*An Enquiry into the Origin of Honour, and the Usefulness of Christianity in War* (1732) and *A Letter to Dion* (1732)—may properly be considered as further additions to the *Fable*. For in the *Enquiry into the*

Origin of Honour Cleomenes and Horatio reappear to continue their earlier discussions, and in *A Letter to Dion* Mandeville defends his book against the charges that had been leveled at it by Bishop Berkeley in his *Alciphron: or, the Minute Philosopher.*[12]

III *The Doctor*

Though Mandeville's works sold well, especially in his later years, it is unlikely that they brought him any substantial income. For the support of his family he was primarily dependent upon his medical practice, and as a doctor he seems to have enjoyed a respectable, though not overwhelming, success. In the preface to the 1711 edition of his *Treatise* Mandeville admits that one of his motives in writing it is to make himself better known, and he informs potential patients that he can be reached through his bookseller. By the 1730 edition, however, he drops this passage, evidently feeling no further need for such direct solicitation. Instead, he has his spokesman, Philopirio, explain that he much prefers to keep his practice small since "I am naturally slow, and could no more attend a dozen Patients in a Day, and think of them as I should do, than I could fly."[13] Perhaps using this statement as his source, Sir John Hawkins, writing in 1787 (see below), reports that Mandeville was never able to attract more than a handful of patients and hence lived in poverty. Hawkins, however, cites no authority for his statement, and what evidence there is suggests that Mandeville was a reputable and reasonably successful doctor. A letter of 1716 from Mandeville to Sir Hans Sloane shows Mandeville in familiar professional consultation with the prominent court physician; and the terms of Mandeville's will, while they do not reflect great wealth, do at least indicate a level of moderate prosperity.

Mandeville's own comments on his medical practice are limited to a few references in the *Treatise.* In choosing to speak through Philopirio (which translates as "Lover of Experience"), Mandeville emphasizes his empirical attitude toward medicine. "What I am against," says Philopirio in a characteristic statement, "is, the Speculative part of Physick, as it is distinct from the Practical, that teaches Men to cure all manner of Distempers in their Closets, without ever seeing a Patient."[14] Throughout the work he reiterates his distrust of speculation divorced from observation. A physician's theories, like those of any scientist, Mandeville feels, can be deemed valid only insofar as they enable him to predict precisely and accurately in specific cases. "I'll give you an infallible Touch-stone to try [a physician] by. If in any acute Distemper whatsoever his Predictions be clear, his answers not doubtful, and what he says be true, you may trust him with all the rest; *si secus, non;* and the more ample and circumstantial his Predictions are, depend upon it, the greater is his Skill."[15]

Mandeville prided himself on being such a doctor, and he was not above puffing himself in print. In a burst of generous enthusiasm Misemedon offers Philopirio-Mandeville the following handsome testimonial:

> I sent for you at first, *Philopirio,* only out of Curiosity, to know your Sentiments concerning the Hypochondriack Passion, without any design of taking your Advice, much less your Medicines ... ; but what you have told me of Physick in general, and the Causes of my Distemper in particular, as well as the Constancy with which I see you still adhere to Observation in the tracing of Nature, and the uncommon method of your reasoning by drawing all your Arguments from the solid Basis of well weigh'd Experience, have alter'd my Resolution, and again conquer'd that Prejudice I have so often taken up against Physick: Wherefore, to shew you how unwilling I am to lose any further time, and with how much resignation to your Skill, and candour, I confide in your Promise; from this moment I commit my self entirely to your Care, without enquiry into your method of Cure, desiring you would let me have this very Night whatever you think proper, with necessary Directions.[16]

IV   *His Character*

Of Mandeville's character and personality very little is known, or at any rate, very little that can be trusted. "Whoever labours under the Publick Odium," Mandeville wrote in his "Essay on Charity and Charity-Schools," "has always Crimes laid to his Charge he never was guilty of...."[17] Predictably, Mandeville in his role as the new Machiavelli became the target of a good deal of personal abuse designed to discredit his *Fable* by picturing its author as a profligate and a subverter of religion. His enemies, evidently deriving their information from nothing more tangible than a frenzied sense of what so "immoral" a writer *must* be like, accused Mandeville (or "Man-

Devil," as a favorite pun had it) of a series of sins which included treason, misanthropy, alcoholism, cruelty, and arrogance.

A less fevered, but scarcely flattering view of Mandeville, was recorded by Sir John Hawkins in a passage (mentioned earlier) in his *Life of Johnson:*

He lived in obscure lodgings in London, and betook himself to the profession of physic, but was never able to acquire much practice. He was the author of the [*Fable of the Bees*], as also of 'Free Thoughts on Religion,' and 'a Discourse on Hypochondriac Affections,' which Johnson would often commend; and wrote besides, sundry papers in the 'London Journal,' and other such publications, to favour the custom of drinking spiritous liquors, to which employment of his pen, it is supposed he was hired by the distillers. I once heard a London physician, who had married the daughter of one of that trade, mention him as a good sort of man, and one that he was acquainted with, and at the same time assert a fact, which I suppose he had learned from Mandeville, that the children of women addicted to dram-drinking, were never troubled with the rickets. He is said to have been coarse and overbearing in his manners where he durst be so; yet a great flatterer of some vulgar Dutch merchants, who allowed him a pension. This last information comes from a clerk of a city attorney, through whose hands the money passed.[18]

Most of Hawkins's allegations are either highly dubious (relying, as they do, on unconfirmed statements from unidentified sources), or else are demonstrably false (as, for example, the accusation that Mandeville was hired by distillers to praise drinking in the *London Journal;* Mandeville neither wrote, nor did the *London Journal* ever print, articles of such a nature).

To Hawkins's secondhand view of Mandeville's coarseness we may add two firsthand allusions to his personality, one which supports Hawkins's estimate, and another which is somewhat more generous. Dr. Charles A. Clarke, writing to a Mrs. Clayton on April 22, 1732, remarks concerning Mandeville and his friendship with the influential Lord Chancellor, the Earl of Macclesfield: "It is probable this gentleman [Mandeville] may be a favourite author with the town, though I am surprised he should be so much in the confidence of a great man who is ambitious of patronizing men of worth and learning, unless he is capable of mistaking low humour and drollery for fine wit."[19] Benjamin Franklin, however, records in his *Autobiography* that in 1725 Dr. Lyons "carried me to the Horns, a pale Ale-House in —— Lane, Cheapside, and introduc'd me to Dr. Mandevile, Author of the Fable of the Bees, who had a Club there, of which he was the Soul, being a most facetious entertaining Companion."[20]

Mandeville died at the age of sixty-three on January 21, 1733. The cause of his death is unknown, though Kaye plausibly conjectures that it may have been the influenza epidemic which contemporary periodicals record as then prevalent. In his will, which is dated April 2, 1729, he bequeathed to his wife one hundred pounds plus certain annuities; and he gave to his daughter, Penelope, twenty-five shillings to pay for a mourning ring. The bulk of his estate he left to his son and executor, Michael, "desiring of him to bury me as near by, and in as private a manner as shall be consistent with the cheapest Decency."[21]

CHAPTER 2

Mandeville's Verse

A S a poet—beginning with the publication in 1703 of *Some Fables After the Easie and Familiar Manner of Monsieur de la Fontaine*—Bernard Mandeville made his first attempts to establish a career as an English author. In the preface to that work we may detect the protective modesty of a writer who fears that the public may not be favorably impressed:

Good Reader; . . . all my Business with you, is, to let you know, that I have writ some Fables in Verse, after the Familiar Way of a Great Man in *France, Monsieur de la Fontaine.* I have confin'd my self to strict Numbers, and endeavour'd to make 'em free and natural; if they prove otherwise I'm sorry for it. Two of the Fables are of my own Invention; but I'm so far from loving 'em the better, that I think they are the worst in the Pack: And therefore in good Manners to my self I conceal their Names. Find 'em out, and welcome. I could wish to have furnish'd you with something more worthy your precious time: But as you'll find nothing very Instructive, so there's little to puzzle your Brain. Besides, I desire every Body to read 'em at the same Hours I writ 'em; that's when I had nothing else to do. If any like these Trifles, perhaps I may go on; if not, you shall be troubled with no more of 'em: And so fare ye well *Reader.*[1]

The contemporary response to *Some Fables* has not been directly recorded, but we may assume that Mandeville did not at first find it unduly discouraging since he reissued the book in 1704 with additions under the title *Aesop Dress'd: Or, A Collection of Fables Writ in Familiar Verse.* He retained his unassuming preface, but added his name (as "B. Mandeville, M.D.") to the title page.

By the time that Mandeville was ready with his second book of verse, however, the reaction to his fables had evidently become so far from flattering that he made public note of it.

Mandeville opens his preface to *Typhon* (1704) by remarking with some asperity:

I presented you some time ago with a Dish of Fables; *but* Wel[ling]ton [Richard Wellington, publisher of *Some Fables* and *Aesop Dress'd*] says, They went down with you like chopt Hay: *Raw, I'm sure, they were very good Meat; and either I have been the Devil of a Cook to 'em, or else your Mouth was out of Taste: if I spoyl'd them in the Dressing, I ask my* French *Caterer's pardon; if not, I know who ought to beg mine. I told you then, that if you did not like them, you should be troubled with no more of 'em, and I have been as good as my word; for I have made no more* Fables *since, than I have built Churches.*[2]

Mandeville risks a similar response to his new book by making the same sort of promise he had offered in introducing his fables—that he would publish no more unless the demand should prove sufficient. Elaborating on his metaphor of the poet-as-chef, he tells the reader: *"Now that I have provided you a little* Ragow *of* Gods, Giants, Pins, Speeches, Stars, Meal-tubs, *and other Nick-nacks all jumbled together* a la Francoise: *If it pleases your Palate, there are Four Messes left behind, which you shall have served up, either all together in one great Dish, or else hot and hot, one after another in little* Mazarines *like this, according as the Maggot shall bite."*[3]

In 1705, Mandeville, despite his earlier assertion that he would make "no more Fables," published *The Grumbling Hive: Or, Knaves Turn'd Honest*, which oddly (in view of its later notoriety) seems to have been largely ignored on its first appearance. Mandeville's own diffident assessment of the poem is contained in the preface he added in 1714:

I do not dignify these few loose Lines with the Name of Poem, that I would have the Reader expect any Poetry in them, but barely because they are Rhime, and I am in reality puzzled what Name to give them; for they are neither Heroick nor Pastoral, Satyr, Burlesque, nor Heroi-comick; to be a Tale they want Probability, and the whole is rather too long for a Fable. All I can say of them is, that they are a Story told in Dogrel, which without the least design of being Witty, I have endeavour'd to do in as easy and familiar a manner as I was able: The Reader shall be welcome to call them what he pleases.[4]

Mandeville's final collection of poetry was published in 1712.

Wishes to a Godson, With Other Miscellany Poems (signed "B.M.") contains neither preface nor apology, but merely twelve brief poems, including the four additional fragments of *Typhon* he had withheld eight years before. *Wishes to a Godson*, like its predecessors, seems to have been received with general indifference.

If Mandeville had ever entertained any serious hopes of winning a reputation as a poet, he must have found discouraging the evident readiness with which readers were willing to accept the author's own deprecation of his poems as artistically negligible. On the whole, posterity has agreed with Mandeville's contemporaries; and, except for *The Grumbling Hive* (whose fame can hardly be ascribed to its quality as a poem), Mandeville's verse is very little read today; but such neglect does not mean, however, that Mandeville's poetry is without interest or merit. Though it would be hard to sustain any large claims for his technical skill as a poet, Mandeville's unpretentiously "easie and familiar" style is capable of considerable satiric vigor. At its best, Mandeville's verse resembles that of his contemporary, Daniel Defoe, in its lively, colloquial expressiveness. But, even at its worst, Mandeville's poetry furnishes an interesting foreshadowing of the qualities and concerns he was to display more fully in his prose works.

In meter and tone, the overwhelming majority of Mandeville's verse falls within the general comic tradition established by Samuel Butler with his immensely popular anti-Puritan satire, *Hudibras* (1663–1678). Butler's thumping iambic tetrameter couplets, multiple rhymes, incongruous diction, and deliberate wrenching of accent had been widely imitated by his successors, though seldom with his felicity. By the early eighteenth century, however, the descriptive term "Hudibrastic" had become broad enough to include almost any eight-syllable, four-stress, satiric couplets which deliberately employed harsh rhyme and low imagery for comic purposes; and it is in such general resemblances (and in tone) that Butler's influence is evident in Mandeville's poetry. For neither Mandeville's usual subject matter nor the nature of his poetic skills lent themselves to the sort of brilliant wit and mechanical virtuosity displayed by the author of *Hudibras*.

Beyond such things as an occasional multiple rhyme clearly based on Butler's example ("Before the Reign of Buxom

Dido, / When Beasts could Speak as well as I do"),[5] Mandeville's most noteworthy technical resemblance to Butler lies
in his fondness for feminine endings, which occur in some
twenty percent of his poetry.[6] The "great Hudibrastic vigour"[7]
which Coleridge praises in the lines on lawyers in *The Grumbling Hive* (ll. 59–70) derives to a far greater extent from their
Butlerian spirit than from their few faint echoes of Butler's
ingenious prosody. It is in such relatively diffuse things as
Mandeville's conversational manner and his irreverently sar-
donic approach that we see him most clearly reflecting the
man he once acknowledged as "the incomparable *Butler.*"[8]

I *The Fabulist*

In turning to the fable for his debut as a poet, Mandeville
was employing a literary mode which could claim a pedigree
as ancient and an appeal as universal as any. There can be
few countries or cultures which have not from earliest times
told stories in which simple characters (frequently animals
or even inanimate objects) act exemplary roles. In England,
besides the Classical tradition of Aesop and Phaedrus, the
form had roots both in popular folklore and in the more sophisticated literary treatments of such authors as Geoffrey Chaucer,
Edmund Spenser, and John Dryden.

However, it was not to this flourishing native tradition that
Mandeville turned in his role as a fabulist. Instead, *Some
Fables After the Easie and Familiar Manner of Monsieur de
la Fontaine,* as its title announces, undertakes to adapt for
an English audience the witty and deceptively simple fables
for which Jean de la Fontaine (1621–1695) had recently won
so much popularity in France. La Fontaine's 239 verse fables,
published between 1668 and 1694, had created a new appreciation of the form's effectiveness as a vehicle for pointed social
and moral commentary. As early as 1693 John Dennis had
rendered ten of La Fontaine's fables into English octosyllabic
couplets and published them in his *Miscellanies in Verse and
Prose.* In neither spirit nor detail, however, is Dennis close
to La Fontaine, whom he nowhere mentions. Far from attempt-
ing to imitate La Fontaine's elegance, Dennis employs a
deliberately broad, comic lowness of style, which, in result,
is much closer to burlesque than to the French original's grace-
ful indirection.

Mandeville's thirty-seven fables based on La Fontaine (twenty-seven in *Some Fables*, plus the ten added a year later in *Aesop Dress'd*) constitute the first book-length version of these works in English. Though Mandeville's renderings come closer to La Fontaine's poems, both in particulars and in tone, than had Dennis's, it would be misleading to consider them simply as "translations," if by that term we imply works which strive to duplicate their originals as accurately as the requirements of a different language will allow. In Mandeville's hands, La Fontaine's fables may not be nearly unrecognizable, as they are in Dennis's, but they have, nevertheless, a character and flavor distinctly different from their originals. Some of this difference, no doubt, is ascribable to Mandeville's lesser skill, as well as to the inevitable incompatabilities of connotation between two languages, especially as reflected by an author to whom neither language is native—though Mandeville's ear for English, at any rate, is usually very accurate.

But to explain the differences between La Fontaine's fables and Mandeville's versions of them primarily in such terms is not really satisfactory, for such an explanation assumes that Mandeville saw himself in the self-effacing role of "translator," and that accordingly his fables can be judged as failures to the extent that they do violence to the originals. Aware perhaps that his poetic talents were much smaller than La Fontaine's, Mandeville seems to have followed Dennis's lead and to have attempted not a translation (a word he conspicuously avoids applying to his fables), but something closer to an "imitation"—a literary mode in which the acknowledged original is more or less freely adapted, with emphasis, allusions, proportions, and treatment altered to fit the imitator's temperament and desired effect.

Mandeville himself describes the process accurately, if ironically, in *The Virgin Unmask'd* (1709), where Lucinda, in discussing the difficulties of translation, cites the following hypothetical case:

Take an *English*-Man, that understands *French* enough to translate from it, with now and then the Help of a Dictionary; suppose him to meet with a celebrated Poem in that Language, being a Stranger to the Elegancy, as well as the Gravity and Easiness of the Diction, all his Aim is, to know what he calls the intrinsick Value of it, the Meaning: So, having roughly hammer'd out the Sense, he likes it

extraordinarily well; but as he ruminates upon it, some witty Flights
jumping into his Head upon the Occasion, he blames the *French*-Man
for not having made the best of so fine a Thought, without considering,
that, according to the different Rules, what may be very *apropos*
in *English*, would have been as unseasonable in the *French*: Inspir'd
by Wit, the Darling of his Country, he resolves upon an Imitation,
and happily renders the Substance of every Thought into good *English*
Verse.[9]

In his preface to *Aesop Dress'd* Mandeville speaks only of
having written his poems *"after the Familiar Way"*[10] of La
Fontaine, thus repeating in slightly different form the phrase
he had used in his title. He nowhere claims to offer a faithful
rendering, and the change in title from *Some Fables After
the Easie and Familiar Manner of Monsieur de la Fontaine*
(1703) to *Aesop Dress'd: Or, A Collection of Fables Writ in
Familiar Verse* (1704) may have been at least partly motivated
by Mandeville's desire to discourage direct comparisons. It
is, nevertheless, illuminating to make such a comparison, for
the specific ways in which Mandeville shapes La Fontaine's
fables to fit his own concerns furnish a convenient framework
within which to explore some of the more noteworthy characteristics of Mandeville's verse.[11]

In his 1668 preface La Fontaine counsels those who might
hope to improve upon his fables: " . . . *il ne sera pas difficile
de donner un autre tour à celles-là même que j'ai choisies;
et si ce tour est moins long, il sera sans doute plus approuvé.*"[12]
The proffered advice in favor of brevity was to be largely
ignored by Mandeville, for the most immediately noticeable
difference between the fables of Mandeville and La Fontaine
is perhaps the discrepancy in size. It is not uncommon to
find Mandeville taking half again as many lines (or, in a few
cases, twice as many) as La Fontaine had required for the
same fable. What La Fontaine's thirty-seven originals present
in a total of 1349 lines, Mandeville expands into 1715 lines.
Part of this discrepancy is due to the greater range of expression
which La Fontaine's variable line lengths allow over the relatively inflexible octosyllabic couplets Mandeville uses. But
metrics can account for only a small percentage of the increase;
the major portion of Mandeville's greater length is the result
of the added detail, commentary, and example by which he

seeks to adapt these poems to his own voice and purpose.

An important factor contributing to La Fontaine's brevity is his policy of merely implying, rather than overtly enunciating, the analogies and moral lessons to be derived from his tales. The reader is either invited to draw the appropriate conclusions from the tale itself or, in those cases where guidance is supplied, the author points the way as unobtrusively as possible. Such restraint, which places a premium upon qualities of concision, understatement, and indirection, is quite foreign to Mandeville, whose whole thrust is toward the explicit. What La Fontaine merely suggests, Mandeville regularly spells out, often as not with accompanying elaboration and illustration. It is noteworthy that in most of Mandeville's fables the moral is labeled as such and segregated from the poem, which is only occasionally the case with La Fontaine.

Thus, in La Fontaine's *"Le Gland et la Citrouille"* (IX, iv), we meet a villager who criticizes God's sense of fitness in placing so imposing a fruit as the pumpkin on a lowly, creeping vine, while the impressive oak tree bears only an insignificant acorn. Falling asleep under the tree, he is awakened when an acorn drops on his nose. After reflecting on what damage a pumpkin might have inflicted, he commends God's wisdom and goes home contentedly, at which point La Fontaine's poem ends. In Mandeville's "The Pumkin and Acorn" there are six additional lines, separated from the text, italicized, and specifically identified as "The Moral."

> *The World's vast Fabrick is so well*
> *Contrived by its Creator's Skill;*
> *There's nothing in't, but what is good*
> *To him, by whom its understood;*
> *And what opposes Human Sence,*
> *Shews but our Pride and Ignorance.* (ll. 31–36)

While this belaboring of the point can hardly be justified as an "improvement" over La Fontaine's less explicit ending, it is possible to understand why Mandeville chose deliberately to limit the possible range of interpretation. La Fontaine, by not enunciating more fully the lesson to be drawn from his tale, has created a certain satiric ambiguity. In La Fontaine's terse fable, the villager's final praise of God's common sense

("*il eut raison;/J'en vois bien à présent la cause*") is scarcely
less fatuous than his earlier carping; and this fact offers a tacit
invitation to an ironic reading beyond the surface moral. Thus,
in La Fontaine's version, in addition to the obvious moral
—"The more we understand of God's great scheme of things,
the more apparent its perfection becomes"—there is a suggested correlate—"Our solemn approval of God's arrangements reflects a vanity just as presumptuous as that which
prompts our criticisms of Him." Mandeville, by firmly telling
us exactly what he wants us to conclude, loses a good deal
in nuance; but he does achieve the sort of unequivocal clarity
of statement that he values.

A subsidiary aspect of Mandeville's efforts to underscore
the moral application of his fables can be seen in the way
he introduces specifically English allusions and attitudes.
These alterations sometimes amount to little more than re-
placing or enhancing La Fontaine's original references with
ones more appropriate to a British audience. Thus, the ass
in La Fontaine's "*Les Animaux malades de la Peste*" (VII,
i) eats the grass in a monastery meadow; in Mandeville's "The
Plague among the Beasts", he stops for his meal in a "Church-
yard" while en route to "*Sturbridge*-Fair." Similarly, while
in La Fontaine's "*La Laitière et le Pot au Lait*" (VII, x) the
narrator explains that in his dream of military glory he pictures
himself as conquering the Emperor of Persia; in Mandeville's
equivalent fantasy: "I beat the *French* in half an Hour,/Get
all their Cities in my Power" (ll. 45–46). Likewise, Mandeville
sometimes adds a specifically English application where La
Fontaine had merely suggested a general one. La Fontaine's
"*Les Grenouilles qui demandent un Roi*" (III, iv) simply concludes that those who experiment with forms of government
may find the replacement worse than the original. To this
Mandeville, in "The Frogs asking for a King," satirically adds:

> *Thank God, this Fable is not meant*
> *To* Englishmen; *they are content,*
> *And hate to change their Government.* (ll. 54–56)

In what is perhaps his most genuinely witty local allusion,
Mandeville introduces Mercury (in "The Woodcleaver and

Mercury") with a description which, for obvious reasons, is absent in La Fontaine's "*Le Bûcheron et Mercure*" (V, i):

> ... *Mercury* the Post-Boy, or
> The Flying Post (his Character
> Suits either for he's God of Lying
> Beardless, and fam'd for News and Flying). (ll. 15–18)

No contemporary English reader would be likely to miss the evenhanded irony at the expense of the rival London political periodicals, the Tory *Post-Boy* and the Whig *Flying Post*.

As can be seen from such examples, one result of Mandeville's penchant for the explicit and the particular is that in his hands the fable's didactic function becomes much more obtrusive than is the case with La Fontaine. Though Mandeville had warned his readers in his preface to expect "*nothing very Instructive*" in the fables, he clearly takes special pains to make the moral point of each tale as forceful and as pointed as he can. In Mandeville's tendency to tell his readers just what to conclude, we may detect in embryo the same didactic impulse which led him in later years to add the immense interpretative apparatus that transformed the twenty-one pages of *The Grumbling Hive* into the 789 pages of *The Fable of the Bees*.

The greater length of Mandeville's fables as compared to La Fontaine's, however, is only partially due to the former's overt moralizing; for Mandeville also seeks, through the copious use of dramatic detail, to delight his readers while instructing them. It is through addition of such details that Mandeville most conspicuously increases the size of La Fontaine's originals, at the same time imposing upon them a new and homier flavor. La Fontaine, by his relatively terse narrative style, aims for what he calls "*la brèveté, qu'on peut fort bien appeler l'âme du conte....*"[13] With such a standard in mind, he selects primarily such details of character, dialogue, and setting as contribute directly to the central point. La Fontaine's fables are not bare of detail or adornment, but the proportion of such peripheral touches is not high.

Mandeville, on the other hand, approaches his fables in the spirit of a gossipy anecdotalist, consciously working to fill out his story with plausible background, comic highlights, and descriptive passages. Such material, when excessively used, can make for prolixity and diffusion; but, as raconteurs have always known, such detail can also add color, humor, and vividness to a narrative. In Mandeville's adaptions, La Fontaine's fables lose much of their classical spareness and restraint, assuming instead a dramatic liveliness more in keeping with Mandeville's own abilities and temperament.

To the charge that his circumstantial embellishments were both low in nature and structurally irrelevant, Mandeville, we may assume, would have replied as he did in a similar situation twenty-two years later. In the preface to *An Enquiry into the Causes of the Frequent Executions at Tyburn* (1725) Mandeville tells critics who object to his inclusion of so much lively, but only marginally relevant description of prison life:

... when a Piece is lively and tolerably finish'd, the good-natured Critick will pardon the Meaness of the Design, for the sake of the Colouring and the Application of the Master [sic]. But if [such explanations are not] thought sufficient, I must plead guilty, and confess that the Pleasure there is in imitating Nature in what Shape soever is so bewitching, that it over-rules the Dictates of Art, and often forces us to offend against our own Judgment.[14]

With Mandeville's augmentations, La Fontaine's sixty-one line *"Le Jardinier et son Seigneur"* (IV, iv) becomes the 115-line "The Countryman and the Knight," and in the process changes from a relatively straightforward parable to a dramatically heightened comic sketch. Of La Fontaine's *"Jardinier"* we learn no more than that he was *"par un lièvre troubleé"* (l. 9); Mandeville in nine lines pictures both the hare's depredations and the "Countryman's" rage:

> Only a Hare wou'd now and then
> Spite of the Master and the Men
> Make raking work for half a day,
> Then fill her Gut and scow'r away.
> In vain they beat and search the Ground,
> The cunning Jilt can ne'er be found,
> The Master once in angry Mood
> Starts up and swears by all that's good,
> He'd be revenged, that he would. (ll. 13–21)

The *"Jardinier"* appeals for help to a nearby lord, who *"vient avec ses gens"* (l. 19). The arrival of the "Knight" who comes to the aid of Mandeville's "Countryman" creates an uproar which takes eight lines to describe. Similarly, whereas La Fontaine tells us little more than that the *"Seigneur"* and his company ate a hearty meal at their host's expense, Mandeville paints a graphic picture of the scene:

> Now all's fetch'd out,
> The Victuals rak'd, and tore about.
> One pairs the Loaf, another Groom
> Draws Beer, as if he was at home,
> And spils [*sic*] it half about the Room.
> What Horseman's yonder at the Door?
> Why, Faith, there's half a dozen more:
> They're Gentlemen, that live at Court,
> Come down the Country for some Sport;
> Some old Acquaintance of the Knight,
> Who whips from Table, bids 'em light.
> They ask no Questions but sit down,
> Fall too [*sic*] as if it were their own.
> One finishes the Potted Salmon,
> Then swears, because he had no Lemon.
> Good Lord, how sharp the Rouges are set! (ll. 40–55)

The *"Seigneur"* in La Fontaine's fable boldly flirts with the *"Jardinier's"* daughter and finally ventures an unspecified *"caresse"* (l. 38); the daughter of Mandeville's "Countryman" must endure not only a "kiss" from the "Knight," but even more indelicate treatment from one of his entourage:

> And now the Knight would let her go;
> Another Rake cries, Damme no:
> I'll have a Kiss as well as you.
> He hugs her close, then calls her Dear,
> And whispers bawdy in her Ear.
> My charming Rogue, I would not hurt ye.
> She answers not, but drops a Courtsie.
> He's rude, and she's asham'd to squeak;
> Her father sees it [,] dares not speak. (ll. 71–79)

When La Fontaine's *"Seigneur"* and his pack set out to catch the hare, the havoc they wreak is not so much depicted as

reflected indirectly in the rueful lament of the watching
"*Jardinier*":

> *adieu planches, carreaux;*
> *Adieu chicorée et porreaux;*
> *Adieu de quoi mettre au potage.* (ll. 44–46)

In Mandeville the process of destruction itself is described:

> Down goes the Quick-set hedge, and Pales.
> The Huntsman hollows, runs and pushes,
> All goes to Rack, the Borders, Bushes,
> And now my Landlord cries amain,
> You've ruin'd me; but all in vain.
> The Cabbages are kick'd about,
> And Flowers with Roots and all pull'd out.
> The Beds are levell'd with the Ground. (ll. 85–92)

At last the hare is taken (in La Fontaine, for additional ironic
effect, he escapes); the hunters depart; and, when, Mandeville
gives the moral, he elaborates characteristically into eight lines
what La Fontaine economically states in four:

> *When petty Princes can't agree,*
> *And strive for Superiority,*
> *They often take my Landlord's Course,*
> *Invite for Aid a foreign Force;*
> *And when their Subjects Slaves are made,*
> *Their Countries all in ruins laid,*
> *As commonly it proves their fate,*
> *Repent with him when it's too late.* (ll. 108–115)

In almost every case in which Mandeville has appreciably
expanded La Fontaine's original fable, we find a similar piling
up of the sort of dramatic and descriptive detail which La
Fontaine either limits to essentials or sketches in obliquely.

In keeping with Mandeville's conversational manner, he
frequently enlivens his dialogue with the sort of slangy col-
loquialism and raciness that occurs only sparingly in La Fontaine's originals. La Fontaine's characters, insofar as we hear
their actual words, are inclined to speak either with an appropriately artless simplicity or with a solemn dignity of tone

that becomes ironic in context. In *"Le Lion et le Moucheron"* (II, ix), La Fontaine makes us smile at the lofty self-assurance with which the lowly gnat responds to the lion's contemptuous dismissal:

> *"Penses-tu, lui dit-il, que ton titre de roi*
> *Me fasse peur ni me soucie?*
> *Un boeuf est plus puissant que toi:*
> *Je le mène à ma fantaisie."* (ll. 5–8)

But when, in Mandeville's "The Lyon and the Gnat," the equivalent speech is rendered, it is the pugnacious sauciness of the gnat, rather than his sang-froid, that amuses:

> ... Bully, Think ye that
> I'll bear Affronts? No: And declar'd
> A War against him to his Beard;
> And told the Hector, void of fear,
> You'll find Sir King, how much I care
> For all your Titles, Tooth and Claw,
> Of which great Loobies stand in awe:
> I'll quickly curb your haughtiness,
> Damn'd Brute.... (ll. 4–12)

That the fable as wielded by Mandeville is an altogether blunter instrument than that which La Fontaine employed will be apparent to even the most casual reader. However, as the foregoing comparisons suggest, the difference is not merely the inadvertent result of imprecise translation. La Fontaine's felicities—his brevity, muted nuance, and understated irony—were as alien to Mandeville's temperament as they were beyond his poetic grasp. Accordingly, he makes no serious attempt to duplicate them, choosing instead to refashion the French originals into a species of loose comic sketch wherein his own taste for overt moralizing, colorful detail, and lively dialogue can be freely indulged. These qualities give Mandeville's fables, at their best, the same sort of ebullient conversational informality that figures so prominently in his prose. On the other hand, these same qualities in excess can result in fables whose focuses become blurred in a haze of narrative embellishments and explications.

It is instructive in this connection to examine the handful

of fables that are of Mandeville's own invention. "The Carp" and "The Nightingale and the Owl" (both of which appeared in *Some Fables)* and *The Grumbling Hive* (published separately a year later) are stories original with Mandeville; and in them, as might be expected, we find displayed in heightened form his major qualities as a fabulist. In "The Carp" Mandeville tells the story of a vain, affected fish who leaves the Thames to travel the great world. Unable to speak any foreign languages, he wanders aimlessly until at last he meets two herrings, who address him in his own language and question him about news of Parliament and the court. Finding that he knows nothing of his own nation's affairs, the herrings dismiss the carp with contempt. He falls in with a debauched pike, who introduces him to the ocean's fleshpots. Finally—diseased and impoverished—the carp returns to his home, no wiser than when he had left it.

Of Mandeville's three original fables, "The Carp" is closest in spirit to La Fontaine's example. Mandeville tells the story in a relatively brief sixty lines, limiting his dramatic detail to a few touches which enhance, rather than interfere, with the effect. In response to the herrings's questions about politics, for example, the carp haughtily replies: "Pish,/... I'm a gentle Fish,/And we know nothing of those Matters" (ll. 27–29). Later, it is a sadly diminished carp whom Mandeville pictures swimming home:

> His Scales begin to drop by scores,
> And all his Body's full of Sores.
> Half of his Tail, and Snout are gone,
> And he, lean, shabby and undone. (ll. 47–50)

Only in delivering the moral of "The Carp" does Mandeville belabor his point, taking eight lines to explain what is already sufficiently obvious from the tale itself—namely, that foreign travel cannot benefit the invincibly vain and ignorant.

In "The Nightingale and Owl," however, Mandeville is much more expansive, and this fable of 181 lines is the largest —by sixty-six lines—of the thirty-nine poems in *Aesop Dress'd.* Part of this length is due to a plot line more involved than that of most fables. The eagle, who is king of the birds, suffers from insomnia and wishes to find some wakeful subject who will serve him through the night. Since none of his courtiers can stay awake, he searches his kingdom for a suitable candidate. The eagle's emissaries approach a nightingale, who is desperately anxious for the job, but whose vanity leads him to act coy and to pretend indifference. Meanwhile, the owl tries out for the job; and, though his song is harsh, his modesty and zeal please the eagle. When at last the nightingale deigns to visit the court, the eagle suggests that the two rivals perform together so that a judgment can be made. The nightingale indignantly refuses to submit to such a contest, and the eagle finally loses his patience. He gives the job to the owl and has the nightingale "punish'd with Disgrace" and "kick'd from Court." The moral, Mandeville tells us, is that men of superior talents may never get the chance to exercise their abilities if, by vanity and insolence, they antagonize the powerful.

In telling this story, Mandeville, as is his usual practice, includes a good deal of graphic material which, if not strictly essential, nevertheless serves a useful function in that it sharpens the satirical delineation of his characters. Thus, we get a seventeen-line account of the nightingale's first reaction to the news about the job opening: in quick succession he is pictured as "almost ready to go mad" with anticipation, as rushing to all his friends to boast of his qualifications, and finally as announcing with transparently false humility that he will not apply for the post, since "Glory's a thing I never went for" (l. 66). Equally full is the scene later in the poem when the nightingale learns from a courtier that the eagle has proposed a singing contest:

> He star'd and cou'd not speak a Word,
> Grew pale, and swell'd, his Wind came short,
> And Anger overwhelm'd his Heart.
> He foams at Mouth, and raves, and blusters,
> And utters all his Words in Clusters.
> A King! a Devil, stupid Fowl,
> That can compare me to an Owl!
> Pray says the Courtier, have a Care,
> Consider in what place you are;
> But, as the Fool would hear no Reason,
> He went, and left him sputt'ring Treason. (ll. 137–147)

While material of this sort adds directly to the central comic

point of the fable, other narrative and descriptive passages
exist whose immediate relevance is questionable. Such a passage occurs, for example, early in the poem, just after the eagle
has decided he needs someone to attend him through the night.
He assembles his courtiers, and for twenty-two lines (or more
than one-ninth of the whole fable) we hear this parliament
of fowls solemnly debate the problem. Each member offers
excuses for his own inability to stay awake and proposes one
or another absurd scheme to insure that whoever is selected
will not sleep on the job. A purist might wonder why so much
time is spent on a scene which has only the remotest bearing
on the moral point of the fable; Mandeville, we may assume,
considered that the intrinsic comedy of the passage sufficiently
justified its inclusion.

The last of Mandeville's original verse fables, *The Grumbling Hive*, is also—at 433 lines—by far the longest one. Mandeville himself, admits in his 1714 preface (quoted earlier)
that "the whole is rather too long for a Fable," and he suggests
that the poem more properly be considered "a Story told in
Dogrel." The length of the poem does not derive from any
particular intricacy of story line. The basic tale of the sinful
but flourishing bees who discover, after their sudden reformation, that moral virtue is not compatible with commercial
prosperity, might easily have been told at a quarter of the
length Mandeville uses. The bulk of *The Grumbling Hive*
comes rather from the wide range and variety of individual
examples wherein Mandeville systematically demonstrates
the specific ways in which private vices can contribute to public benefits. The taste for illustrative embellishment that had
earlier led Mandeville to expand La Fontaine's fables is here
so freely indulged that the result is a work significantly different in scope from the relatively brief and uncomplicated allegory one associates with the traditional verse fable. But the
difference involves more than a simple increase in size and
range; for the very explicitness which commends *The Grumbling Hive* as a survey of society helps to undercut its character
as a fable—and it is a fable (despite Mandeville's misgivings
over classification) that the poem purports to be.

Basic to the appeal of any beast fable is the reader's sense
of the comic incongruity of animals performing in human roles.
Far from diminishing the applicability of the allegory, the spec-

tacle of beasts behaving like men can add a valuable dimension of irony to a story which might, if told in soley human terms, be a simple, nonsatiric parable. But the fabulist, unless he wishes to be deliberately farcical, must take care that the actions of his characters do not become so explicitly or exclusively human as to be grossly at odds with their animal natures. A long-established convention, for example, has made the lion an appropriate symbol for a human king; but the careful fabulist will try to see to it that most of his lion's actions are suitably leonine analogues—rather than incongruously exact reproductions—of the human behavior being allegorized. Thus, the decorum of the fable requires that the lion who is depicted as holding royal court will do so in a cave, as opposed to a palace, and that if he kills an opponent in battle, he will use his teeth and claws—not a sword or pistol. As the example of *The Grumbling Hive* demonstrates, the more precisely detailed his allegory is, the likelier it is that the fabulist will produce animals who, instead of serving as counterparts to men, become simply human characters arbitrarily designated by animal names.

Early in *The Grumbling Hive* Mandeville gives his readers clear notice that he will not even attempt the difficult task of inventing bee equivalents for the wide range of human behavior he wishes to discuss. Of his "Spacious Hive well stockt with Bees," he says:

> These Insects liv'd like Men, and all
> Our Actions they perform'd in small:
> They did whatever's done in Town,
> And what belongs to Sword or Gown:
> Tho' th' Artful Works, by nimble Slight
> Of minute Limbs, 'scap'd Human Sight;
> Yet we've no Engines, Labourers,
> Ships, Castles, Arms, Artificers,
> Craft, Science, Shop, or Instrument,
> But they had an Equivalent:
> Which, since their Language is unknown,
> Must be call'd as we do our own. (ll. 13–24)

In the remainder of the work Mandeville treats his bees

in exclusively human terms, and, accordingly, his poem functions as a fable only in the loosest sense. Instead, it emerges
as a straightforward exemplary tale whose perfunctory trap-
pings as a fable remain mostly irrelevant and at times jarringly
incongruous. In effect, Mandeville requires that his readers
forget that the characters are bees at all, though throughout
the poem he regularly refers to them as such. The reader of
The Grumbling Hive who tries to visualize these "Bees" will
find his ingenuity strained, for he will be obliged to imagine
them in some startlingly unbeelike postures and pursuits.
Among other things, they work as "Pick-pockets" (l. 50), have
their "Limbs shot off" in battle (l. 104), sit in the pillory (l.
147), execute their criminals by hanging (l. 148) or by the
headsman's ax (l. 271), wear gloves made of lamb's skin (l.
221), use "Inkhorns" (l. 259), ride coaches drawn by horses
(ll. 324–25), and employ decorative stone-cutters to adorn their
houses (l. 354). After such information, it comes as something
of a shock at the end of the poem to hear that the bees, having
decided to resettle their diminished population, "flew into
a hollow Tree" (l. 407).[15]

It is perhaps only the overly literal reader who will be much
disturbed by such matters, but we may still wonder why, since
Mandeville's bees are never pictured as such, he bothered
to introduce them into the poem at all. There is, of course,
a certain satiric point implicit in the very idea of representing
men as insects; but, by begging off the job of inventing bee
equivalents for human activities, Mandeville chooses not to
make that point central, and in so doing he reduces the whole
concept of human society as a bee hive to little more than
a general metaphor serving no important allegorical purpose
in the poem. In pointing this out, I do not mean to imply
that *The Grumbling Hive* would have been "improved" had
Mandeville decided to present bee analogues for all the varied
human roles his characters fill. Such a job not only would
have been immensely difficult but would almost inevitably
have created so great an emphasis on far-fetched entomology
as to divert attention from the survey of human society that
is Mandeville's central theme. On the whole, the example of
The Grumbling Hive suggests that the verse fable as a genre
does not really lend itself to the sort of complex treatment
of economic, social, and philosophical questions that had by
1705 become Mandeville's major literary concern; and it is

no surprise to find that, after *The Grumbling Hive*, he chose
to abandon the form entirely.

II Typhon *and* Wishes to a Godson

In the sizeable fragment entitled *Typhon: Or, the Wars Between the Gods and Giants: A Burlesque Poem in Imitation of the Comical Mons. Scarron* (1704), Mandeville turned again,
as he had in his fables, to a French literary model. Though
burlesque and travesty had their earlier antecedents, especially in Renaissance Italy, the vogue for these forms in late
seventeenth- and early eighteenth-century England derived
more immediately from the example of Paul Scarron (1610–
1660). Scarron's *Typhon ou la Gigantomachie* (1644) and his
Virgile Travesti (1648–1652) had helped to popularize, first
in France and later in post-Restoration England, that form
of verse in which the language, conventions, and characters
of heroic verse were systematically ridiculed.

Both the travesty (which mocks a specific literary model)
and the burlesque (which parodies a general style or manner)
share incongruity as their basic comic device. A dignified or
serious subject is treated with coarse diction, comically low
dialogue, grotesque imagery, jarring anachronism, and whatever else will serve to render it absurd. Thus, in Scarron's
Typhon the gods and goddesses of Greek mythology are pictured as grossly lascivious seventeenth-century French bourgeoisie, and in his *Virgile Travesti* Aeneas emerges as a dim-witted and lachrymose bumbler.

It is important to distinguish between such burlesque and
the mock-heroic mode which flourished in the same period,
for the satiric intentions of the two genres are quite different.
The mock-heroic, as in Nicolas Boileau's *Lutrin* (1674), John
Dryden's *MacFlecknoe* (1682), Samuel Garth's *Dispensary*
(1699), and Alexander Pope's *Rape of the Lock* (1714), normally
undertakes to treat a low or trivial subject in the inappropriately
lofty language and conventions of the Classical epic. The comedy—which arises from the discrepancy between the lowly
subject matter and the dignity of the treatment—is almost never
at the expense of the Classical authors whose diction and mannerisms are employed; instead, the reader is invited to laugh
at the conspicuously prosaic subjects who fall so far short of
the Classical heroes whose memory the poet's language
evokes.

In the burlesque and the travesty, on the other hand, the technique is reversed; and, as a consequence, the satiric thrust takes on an altogether different direction. When a traditionally dignified subject is debased by a deliberately crude caricature of the techniques of serious heroic verse, the resultant ridicule extends beyond the immediate subject and embraces not only the heroic poets whose works are parodied but, by implication, the very concept of heroic verse itself. The echoes of the *Aeneid* in Pope's *Rape of the Lock* are meant only to deflate Belinda's pretenses to dignity, not those of Aeneas, and still less those of Virgil; but in Scarron's *Virgile Travesti* the central target becomes the Latin poet himself and by extension the whole tradition of the Classical past as heroically ideal. As Mandeville puts it in *Typhon:*

> History
> Equals Heroick Poetry
> In loving Lies; some say she uses
> More of 'em, than all th'other Muses. (ll. 669–672)

Scarron's earliest English imitator was Charles Cotton, who in 1660 published his *Scarronides,* a travesty of Book I of *The Aeneid,* to which in 1667 he added an equivalent version of Book IV. In 1665, there appeared anonymously the *Gyants War with the Gods,* a translation of Scarron's *Typhon* sometimes ascribed to John Phillips. However inferior in wit and skill these works were to those of Scarron, they achieved a quick popularity; and what one disapproving critic calls "the pernicious weed" of travesty soon began to flourish in England.[16] In 1665, J. Scudamore published a travesty of the first book of the *Iliad* under the title *Homer a la Mode,* and Ovid was ridiculed in 1673 in the anonymous *Ovid Exulans.* Cotton turned to Lucan in 1675 with his *Scoffer Scoft, or Lucan Burlesqued.* The *Maronides,* John Phillips's translation of the fifth and sixth books of *Virgile Travesti,* appeared in 1678. Such works were followed by numerous other travesties and burlesques in the final decades of the seventeenth century; but, by 1704, when Mandeville published his *Typhon,* the fashion had already begun to subside in response to the more various sorts of humor offered by hudibrastic and mock-heroic verse.

Mandeville's *Typhon* is indebted to Scarron for little more than its subject and general comic approach. The occasional

verbal resemblances seem to derive not so much from conscious imitation as from the almost inevitable similarities to
be expected from two burlesque versions of the same story.
Typhon (or Typhoeus) figures in mythology as the leader of
the Titans, the race of giants who challenge the authority of
Jove. The fury of Typhon's initial onslaught is so great (he
uses whole mountains as missiles) that Jove and the other
gods are obliged to flee from Olympus to Egypt, where they
disguise themselves as animals. Eventually the gods return,
and in a second battle Jove first stuns Typhon with a thunder-
bolt and then confines him to Tartarus, the great abyss at the
bottom of Hades, where his periodic struggles to escape still
produce earthquakes. Scarron's comic version of these events
covers two thousand three hundred lines divided into five
cantos. Mandeville's *Typhon* seems to have been conceived
with a similar plan of organization in mind, though Mandeville
was to abandon it after completing only the 972 lines (the
equivalent of Scarron's 486-line Chant I) that he published
in 1704, plus the four brief fragments (totaling 160 lines) that
appeared in *Wishes to a Godson* (1712).

Mandeville establishes the burlesque's necessary tone of
brisk irreverence very early in his *Typhon,* for he opens by
announcing the subjects he will *not* treat. His work, he explains, deals with neither Aeneas ("... the burnt-out pious
Lad,/So fam'd for carrying of his Dad"—ll. 3–4), Adam ("...
him that lost a Rib a sleeping,/And died for tasting of a Pip-
pin"—ll. 7–8), nor Ulysses ("... that cunning Spark, whose
Tongue/They'd make us believe was so well hung"—ll. 11–12),
but rather with the mighty Typhon. After an unceremonious
invocation of the Muses ("Let's know the truth, good Lass-
es"—l. 61), Mandeville is ready to begin his story. In the original legend, Typhon's motive for attacking the Olympians had
been to avenge an earlier defeat the Titans had suffered at the
hands of Jove. In Mandeville's burlesque, the conflict is provoked by more immediate and much homier circumstances.
On a Sunday afternoon Typhon and his fellow giants decide
to play at nine-pins, using the stone pins and balls Typhon has
fashioned from mountains. During the game a ball accidentally
strikes Typhon, who in his agony picks up all the pins and
flings them into the sky with such tremendous force that they
travel all the way to Olympus. Before the pins reach Olympus,

however, Mandeville takes us there to picture the peaceful
scene their arrival will shortly interrupt.

In the palace kitchen (whose strong smells and numerous
seats suggest to Mandeville "a cleanly House of Office"), Mercury is busy "Dusting with an old Wing of his" (l. 256). Next
door in the dining room Jove and the other Olympians are
sleeping off the effects of the previous night's drunken revelry.
This quiet scene is brusquely interrupted when the first of
Typhon's bowling pins comes crashing through the premises.
The gods, rudely awakened, start up in alarm; and, with the
arrival of the rest of the pins, there is a sort of chain reaction,
by which each of the gods suffers one or more painful indig-
nities. Thus, Vulcan's pipe is violently shattered, spilling hot
coals on the half-naked Juno; her sudden movement over-
throws the bench on which Mars is lying, and as he reaches
out to steady himself, he turns upon his own head a huge
pot of wine, all of which so frightens Minerva's owl that it
sinks its talons into Bacchus's nose.

When Jove learns that Typhon is responsible for what has
happened, he summons Mercury and tells him to seek out
the Titans and to inform Typhon that, unless he makes restitu-
tion, there will be a terrible revenge. Mercury sets out at once,
stopping for only a brief rest at Helicon, where the Muses
quiz him for details of the latest gossip ("We've heard, that
that bold Trollop *Venus*/Had Clapt the good Old Man
Silenus"—ll. 681–682). Before replying, Mercury takes a drink
from Hypocrene, which inspires in him a declamation so rap-
turously "poetic" that even the Muses find it intolerably bom-
bastic. Continuing his journey, Mercury at last reaches the
camp of the Titans and delivers his message. Typhon responds
with a coarsely abusive speech in which he characterizes Jove
as a whoremonger and Mercury as his pimp. At this point,
Book I concludes; and, except for the four brief fragments
of a projected Book II finally published in 1712 ("A Description
of Morning," "The Speech of *Bacchus*," "The Speech of
Neptune," and "The Encounter between *Mars* and *Encelade*")
Mandeville carried the work no further.

From the above summary of Book I, it should be apparent
that Mandeville's *Typhon* proceeds with a considerable, if
rather slap-dash, comic energy, though the poem suffers from
certain limitations inherent in Mandeville's approach to bur-

lesque. *Typhon*, like any burlesque, relies largely upon shock effect for its comedy. The reader is startled into laughter by the incongruous spectacle of Olympians acting and speaking in a manner appropriate to Cockney vulgarians, but only so many variations can be played upon this basic comic device before it begins to wear thin. An added dimension of comedy may be achieved if the author chooses to burlesque not merely the actions and characters of heroic verse, but also the particular literary technique and mannerisms of such verse.

In Scarron's *Typhon*, for example, the "author" is almost as much a comic personage as the characters he describes. He frequently digresses to explain the difficulties of doing justice to his subject; he interrupts his story to indulge in mock-pedantic precision over absurdly trivial details; and he ridicules, by artfully maladroit imitations, such epic conventions as the extended simile and the catalogue of heroes. Parody of this sort is not altogether lacking in Mandeville's *Typhon*, but he seems a good deal more interested in debunking the *heroes* of mythology than in satirizing the literary methods of heroic verse.

When Mandeville's Mercury drinks from Hypocrene, for example, he becomes

> Fill'd ... with so much Poetry,
> That having a large stock of Wit,
> And not the Judgment requisite
> To curb it, in continued flight
> He talked like unshav'd *Bedlamite*. (ll. 694–98)

Mandeville goes on for twenty-one lines to describe how Mercury's "Poetick Frenzy" filled the air with fustian, but nowhere does he exploit the opportunity for literary parody by giving an example of the declamation itself. As a result, Mandeville's ridicule in this passage falls more heavily upon Mercury himself than upon the sort of poetic nonsense ostensibly under attack. The promise of Mandeville's preface that he will give his readers "Gods no wiser than some of us" is amply fulfilled. But the comic possibilities of such an approach are soon exhausted, and we sense that Mandeville's eventual abandonment of the work may have been as much due to his own ennui as to lack of public encouragement.

Wishes to a Godson, With Other Miscellany Poems (1712)

has about it the air of a work thriftily designed to use up the unpublished odds and ends remaining in the author's poetry notebook. Besides the four additional fragments of *Typhon*, the collection contains only eight poems, the longest of which is the 117-line title-piece. In the latter, Mandeville's hopes for his godson's future health and prosperity are enlivened by a series of less conventional wishes ("May your Whores be prudent, true,/And Coquets to all but you").[17]

"To Madame N.," "Leanders excuse to *Cloris*," "The yeilding [sic] Minute," and "On *Celia*'s Bosom" are wittily cynical love poems in the manner of Matthew Prior. "A Letter to Mr. *Asgil*" ridicules the eccentric theology of John Asgill (1659–1738), who in 1699 had published a pamphlet arguing that death of the body need not be a prerequisite for entry into heaven. Anticipating a later theme of Mandeville's, "On Honour" pictures the goddess as a cold-hearted enchantress who lures men to ruin by the promise of imaginary rewards. The last poem in the collection is the Latin *"In senem lippum & Asthmaticum, qui annos Sexaginta natus uxorem duxit, & gladio se cinxit inassuetus."* Based on Ovid's *Amores* (I, 9), Mandeville's poem mocks a bleary-eyed, wheezing old man who has just married a young girl.

At the outset of his career as a poet—in the preface to his fables—Mandeville had spoken with scorn of those authors who display greater art in the introductions to their works than in the works themselves. The result, says Mandeville, frequently resembles "a rich piece of Filligrew Work over the Door of an empty Parlour."[18] It is an irony Mandeville himself would have appreciated that, in the poems which follow, there is little to match the vigor and expressiveness of the prose in the prefatory remarks. But, in the decade which followed, public indifference to his poetry and an increasing awareness of the direction in which his literary abilities lay gradually persuaded Mandeville to abandon verse in favor of the essay and the dialogue. Free of the constraints imposed by meter and rhyme, Mandeville could fully cultivate the conversational informality, colorful detail, and careful explication which contribute so much to the effectiveness of his prose; and, after 1712, except for the few lines of verse interspersed in some of his prose works, Mandeville published no other poetry.

CHAPTER 3

The Virgin Unmask'd

A S a result perhaps of the discouraging reception accorded to Mandeville's early efforts in verse, a somewhat tentative air surrounds the issuance of his first work in English prose.[1] In *The Virgin Unmask'd: or, Female Dialogues Betwixt an Elderly Maiden Lady and Her Niece* (1709) Mandeville preserves a semianonymity by leaving his name off the title page, though the preface is signed "B.M."[2] In that preface, just as he had in the introduction to *Some Fables* and to *Typhon,* Mandeville presents his work on a take-it-or-leave-it basis, professing disdain for those authors who try, either by self-praise or mock-humility, to cajole their readers into a favorable frame of mind. Moreover, he repeats an earlier tactic by leaving the work unfinished, thus suggesting (though this time without actually saying so) that its completion is contingent upon how well the initial offering is received. As with *Typhon,* however, readers evidently failed to rise to the bait; and Mandeville's implied continuation never materialized.

In casting *The Virgin Unmask'd* as a dialogue, Mandeville turned to the form which was to remain a favorite throughout the rest of his literary career. For an author with a taste and talent for the lively, the colloquial, and the anecdotal, there are obvious advantages to the dialogue. Its informality of structure, its interplay of ideas and personalities, and its dramatic immediacy are all features particularly suited to Mandeville's skills. There is yet another quality of the dialogue that would recommend it to a writer who so frequently dealt with subjects and viewpoints of an unconventional sort: as opposed to the essay, the dialogue places its author at a certain protective distance from his audience. Unless the author of a dialogue chooses to acknowledge an identity between himself and one of his characters, the reader can never be sure whether what is said represents the writer's opinion or merely that of his fictional creation. The author can thus, without overtly committing himself, forcefully expound ideas whose expression in direct terms might be impolitic. Yet any author knows that, despite his claims to detachment, the natural tendency of readers will be to identify the author's spokesman as that character whose opinions carry the day or whose personality is made especially vivid and attractive. While this commonsensical approach is no doubt valid enough in most cases, it can prove misleading if the author chooses, as Mandeville does in *The Virgin Unmask'd*, to lay a series of traps for the unwary.

The two characters whose conversations comprise the ten brief dialogues of *The Virgin Unmask'd* are Lucinda, the wealthy elderly maiden lady of the title, and her pretty nineteen-year-old niece, Antonia. Lucinda has from an early age been an outspoken hater of men and consequently of marriage, which she sees as a form of bondage for women. She has done her best to instill the strictest principles of chaste behavior upon her ward Antonia, whose parents died some years before. Having herself renounced men forever and hoping to convince her niece to do the same, Lucinda is distressed by what she interprets as the younger woman's growing immodesty. Though Lucinda's attitudes toward sex are uncompromisingly puritanical, she is not a prude nor, oddly enough, is she ill-informed about sexual matters. Her conversation reveals her as a shrewdly observant, obviously intelligent woman who disdains euphemism and who argues her convictions with genuine skill and ingenuity. Though Antonia, who is understandably reluctant to embrace her aunt's philosophy, regularly offers whatever verbal and emotional resistance she can, she has neither eloquence nor knowledge enough to counter Lucinda; and, as a result, Antonia spends much more time listening than she does speaking.

The opening speech of the dialogue is well-calculated to arouse the reader's attention, as Lucinda announces: "Here, Niece, take my Handkerchief, prithee now, if you can find nothing else to cover your Nakedness: If you knew what a Fulsome Sight it was, I am sure you would not go so bare: I cann't abide your Naked Breasts heaving up and down; it makes me Sick to see it."[3] When Antonia petulantly remarks that she does not see why she should be obliged to go around veiled, her aunt crisply tells her that "there is abundance of difference between veiling, and going bare-ass'd" (3). Flaunting the bosom, maintains Lucinda, is little better than obscenity; and she says that her niece reminds her of a merchant who, after boldly parading his goods for the inspection of prospective buyers, may sometimes find himself forced to part with his shopworn merchandise at bargain prices. Stung by this analogy, Antonia pertly replies:

I could say, that when People of Skill like the Goods, they matter but little what Spightful Neighbours speak against them; that Old Traders commonly envy Young Ones; that instead of assisting them, and wishing them well, they endeavour to undermine their Credit, and blow 'em up, if they can. . . . I could say, that they often maliciously give an Ill Name to New Beginners for no other Reason, than to blast their Reputation, and undervalue their Commodities only to spoil a good Bargain. (13)

Lucinda coldly denies the imputed envy, and the first dialogue ends with Antonia retreating to her room in tears.

The conversation resumes later the same day when tempers have calmed. Lucinda comments sadly on the change she has noted in Antonia's attitude toward men. As a child, the niece had seemed to share her aunt's hatred of men; but at fifteen she suddenly became clothes-conscious, learned to dance, and even showed signs of flirting. The process has continued until now, at nineteen, Antonia seems less likely than ever to follow Lucinda's example of renouncing men and marriage forever. The prospect of Antonia's marriage distresses Lucinda not only because (as she readily admits) she is loath to lose her niece's companionship but because a life of misery is inevitable for the woman who lets herself become the "prey" of men.

Lucinda is perfectly aware that few young ladies wish to remain maidens for life, but she maintains that, if one were to question older and wiser married women, not one in five hundred would be without deep regrets over having wed. An equivalent survey of maiden ladies, on the other hand, would reveal that the vast majority (once the "troublesome Itch" of sexual appetite had passed) are well-pleased about having preserved their independence. As a test, Lucinda asks Antonia to name any no longer youthful married woman whose life

seems enviable. Antonia chooses Aurelia, a local widow of
ample fortune whose daughter has married well and whose
later years have been graced by healthy, adoring grand-
children. Lucinda, who knows Aurelia's personal history very
well, promises to tell it in detail the next day.

The third, fourth, and fifth dialogues are Lucinda's caution-
ary account of the life of the seemingly fortunate Aurelia. As
the beautiful sixteen-year-old daughter of a prosperous leather-
seller, Aurelia spurned the deformed but wealthy suitor her
father favored; instead, she fell passionately in love at first
sight with the dashing Dorante, who claimed to be the pro-
prietor of an extensive estate in Ireland. When her father
would not allow the match, Aurelia eloped with Dorante to Ireland which caused her father to renounce her forever.

In Dublin, Aurelia soon learned that Dorante's fortune was
imaginary. Moreover, once it was clear that Aurelia would
bring him no money, Dorante became at first cold, then surly,
and finally brutal toward his now unwanted wife. After two
unhappy years of marriage (and two children), Dorante saw
a chance to salvage some profit from his wife, who had aroused
the interest of a powerful lord from whom Dorante hoped
to win patronage. By various ruses, Dorante tried to lure the
innocent Aurelia into sleeping with his friend, even going
so far as to lock the two of them in a bedroom, where "His
Lordship ... not finding himself in a Condition of going
through the Fatigues of a Rape" (68), finally lost interest.

Bitter with disappointment and desperate for money, Dorante thereafter forced Aurelia to serve as a household drudge
for her shrewish mother-in-law. On his occasional visits home,
he would beat her with insane violence. One such beating
so frightened Aurelia's young son (who witnessed it) that he
fell into fits and died. Some four months later, Aurelia received
the "Joyful Tiddings" of Dorante's death in a duel with a
man whom he had cheated, but soon thereafter she and her
infant daughter were turned out by the mother-in-law. Just
when things were at their blackest for the penniless Aurelia,
she was approached by an emissary of an elderly distant
relative, who asked her to stay with him in London, offering
to give her a handsome dowry if she should some day decide
to marry again. "But *Aurelia*'s Teeth were too much set
on edge, to Bite again in that sour Apple" (108), so she grate-

fully accepted his offer of support, but informed him that she had had her fill of marriage. Upon her benefactor's death a few years later, Aurelia inherited all his money; and since then she has lived in the quiet prosperity which so mistakenly arouses the envy of those who do not know her real story. Antonia, who has been entranced by the tale, comments: "There is Variety enough in her Life, to make a Novel of" (109).

As the conversation resumes the next day, Antonia admits that she had been hasty in choosing Aurelia as an example of one who found happiness in marriage. However, Aurelia's daughter—now twenty-five, beautiful, married for love to a rich and handsome man, and with two bright and healthy children—seems the very model of domestic bliss. Lucinda concedes nothing as she points out the future calamities (deformed children, lost affections, financial disaster, and so on) that lie in wait to spoil even the happiest of marriages. To Antonia's rueful comment: "Aunt, you are enough to Ruine, and unpeople a Common-Wealth" (116), Lucinda responds with an extended comparison between the effects of pregnancy and those of poisoning, both of which, she points out, produce such symptoms as nausea, vomiting, swelling, bleeding, and —in severe cases—death. "Does it not come up to Demonstration, that the Sting of Man comes up to that of the *Tarantula*?" (121). The sexual appetite which induces women to accept such dreadful suffering, says Lucinda, is analogous to the morbid impulse that leads children to eat dirt. Men as a class, she maintains, resemble Louis XIV of France— powerful, intelligent, capable, and terribly dangerous.

When the two women meet again the next morning, Antonia announces to her aunt that no seducer, unless he resorts to actual rape, can ever succeed with a truly virtuous woman. But Lucinda replies that the treachery and ingenuity of men are such that even the most exemplary woman may fall into their traps. To illustrate her point, Lucinda tells the story of Leonora, who was deeply in love with Cleander. Cleander's father, who opposed the match, sent his son to Smyrna and later arranged that Cleander and Leonora should each be informed that the other had died. At first, Leonora's grief was terrible; but, after much time had passed, she accepted the loss and eventually married the worthy but unexciting Al-

candor. A few years later Cleander returned to England, and
when he learned that Leonora was alive, he immediately went
to her. Their love was at once rekindled, but so strict was
Leonora's sense of virtue that she refused to see Cleander
again lest her passions tempt her toward sin. Heart-broken,
Cleander left England and was never heard from again.

Leonora's scrupulous rectitude was all the more praise-
worthy, Lucinda points out, since her easy-going husband was
neither jealous nor even concerned about her relations with
other men. However, the real test of Leonora's virtue came
when, after five years of marriage, she attracted the attention
of the crafty Mincio. Recognizing that a frontal assault would
never work, Mincio pretended to ignore Leonora; instead, he
ingratiated himself with her husband; and he succeeded so
well that the unsuspecting Alcandor finally invited him to
become a permanent house guest.

Far from taking open advantage of this proximity to his prey,
Mincio behaved with great propriety and ingenuity. He
avoided being alone with Leonora, was formally polite in all
his dealings with her, and began to feign a profound sadness
whose cause he refused to discuss. As his pretended gloom
deepened, Mincio finally took to his bed, made out his will,
and gave every evidence of being on the verge of death.
Leonora, who was in great distress over the seemingly afflicted
Mincio, went to his bedside, where his piteous sighs and
glances made her suspect that his decline might have been
due to hopeless love for her. To her tender inquiry, the
"infernal Hypocrite" answered:

Yes, Leonora, . . . *I love you, and for that love I die! Beware of pittying
me, for fear you might insensibly be drawn into my Crime, which
would torment me more than all my present Sufferings; for tho'
I am guilty, yet in the Height of all my Passion, I never wish'd
you so; and I so much admire the Beauties of your Mind, beyond
those of your Body, that had I yet a thousand Lives, I'd lose them
all before you should your Vertue.* (214)

At this crucial juncture, with Leonora facing a choice between
preserving her honor or precipitating the death of the seemingly moribund Mincio, Lucinda interrupts her story, promising that she will conclude it the next day, and on this teasing
note *The Virgin Unmask'd* ends.

I *"Diverting Discourses"*

As should be apparent even in a summary, Mandeville has given his pill of instruction an ample sugarcoating of entertainment. Knowing that the structure of the dialogue form makes it natural for readers to approach the work as they would a species of closet drama, Mandeville has presented his material in a manner designed to heighten the resemblance. Thus, though there are no direct descriptions of the settings (drawing room, summer house, and garden) in which Lucinda and Antonia carry on their conversations, Mandeville usually sets the scene by having one or the other of the women volunteer a few appropriately descriptive references.

Also suggestive of a play is the scenelike division of the work into ten brief dialogues—none self-contained, but each dramatically building upon what has preceded it. Moreover, like a playwright Mandeville rings the curtain down on each of his scenes at precisely the moment best calculated to inspire interest in the next. Dialogue One finishes with Antonia in tears over Lucinda's criticisms; Dialogue Two ends with the promise of Aurelia's sad story; Dialogue Three closes just as Dorante is formulating the arrangements whereby his friend is to rape Aurelia; and so on down to the very conclusion of the book itself on a suspenseful note obviously intended to whet the audience's appetite for a second act. In dramatic terms, the interpolated stories of Aurelia and Leonora act as subplots whose theatrical extravagance augments and enlivens the mostly verbal action of the main dialogue.

Yet, if *The Virgin Unmask'd* had nothing to recommend it but its framework of rudimentary (though effective) dramatic techniques noted above, it would be far less fresh and readable than it is. The exuberance of invention, the fondness for vivid detail, and the sharp ear for colloquial speech that Mandeville had shown in his earlier works are here displayed to much fuller advantage than was possible within the uncongenial restrictions imposed by verse. The result is a work whose appeal is immensely enhanced by the liveliness of its prose and by the variety of its illustrative asides. At one point in her narrative of Aurelia's life, Lucinda stops to ask if perhaps Antonia may not be bored by an account "so particular in Circumstances, that are immaterial to the Plot, and foreign from the End to which a Story is told" (42). Antonia answers that such detail, far from being tedious, is of the greatest interest, and she begs her aunt to continue: "But pray don't be more concise; for it is so entertaining, I am afraid I shan't have enough of it" (43). Antonia's opinion is altogether understandable, for nowhere does *The Virgin Unmask'd* come more fully to life than in its incidental touches.

As background to the story of Aurelia, for example, we learn that her early education was at a wealthy boarding school; and, in Lucinda's jaundiced comments on such establishments, Mandeville gives us an amusingly satiric vignette of the life and behavior of eighteenth-century school-girls:

They lead Easie and Lazy Lives, and have abundance of Time upon their Hands, especially those whose Relations are rich and foolish enough to furnish them with as much Money as may enable them to bribe their Teachers to neglect their Duty, and wink at their Faults, and by cramming themselves with Custards and Cheescakes all Day long, oblige their Mistress with having no Stomach to their Dinner. I have often taken notice, how they have run together in Shoals, whispering and hugging one another, and standing still between whiles, all at once set up a Laughter with so much Loudness, and so many Grimaces, as if they were tickled to Death; and all this occasioned by some silly, naughty Word, they have got by the end; perhaps a baudy Monosyllable, such as Boys write upon Walls.... (48–49)

Even within the conventionally melodramatic confines of the stories of Aurelia and Leonora, Mandeville has included much realistic detail. The love-stricken daughters, irate fathers, ogre husbands, and scheming seducers who appear almost interchangeably in such romances are literary stereotypes borrowed from an already hoary tradition, but Mandeville has endowed them with a more than customary plausibility of speech and psychology. Thus, in describing Dorante's plan to trade Aurelia's body for patronage from a powerful lord, Mandeville has imaginatively entered Dorante's mind and tried to depict in humanly believable terms just how such a man might behave in such a situation. At first, Dorante, who tries an indirect approach, cajoles his wife by flattery, presents, and loud protestations of his own lack of jealousy. When the naive Aurelia, not understanding her husband's drift, politely rejects the advances of the amorous lord, Dorante changes his tactics; he now harangues his bewildered wife with shrill rhapsodies about the innocent pleasures of adultery.

When this tactic also fails, Dorante—who has by now worked himself up to near frenzy—becomes brutally direct. Fortified with alcohol to bolster his courage and to stifle any lingering scruples, he abusively upbraids Aurelia for the financial drain she has been to him and says he will throw her out with her children unless she sleeps with his friend. When Aurelia refuses in horror, Dorante becomes increasingly hysterical in his threats, rationalizations, and blustering self-pity. With the arrival (by previous arrangement) of the would-be rapist, Dorante runs out of the room, pausing only long enough to cry out with a grotesque pretense to gaiety: "there lyes a Foolish Carrion, that has been Crying this half Hour, and I can't tell you for what; She's very ticklish under the short Ribs, I wish your Lordship would try if you can't make her Laugh" (66).

Mandeville's concern for the psychology and motivation of his characters is also apparent in the sequel to these events. Lucinda explains that after Dorante's plans had been thwarted, he took to beating Aurelia regularly, which gradually transformed her former love for him into hatred. When Antonia expresses surprise that Aurelia's hatred did not begin at the very moment Dorante openly ordered her to sleep with another man, Lucinda responds with the following intricate analysis:

Had I been telling you a Romance, I would have made use of Art. . . . But in a true Story, we must relate things as they happen. *Aurelia* was not a Bold Blustering Woman; she was of a meek and quiet Temper; and, for this Reason, the first Passion it raised in her, was her Sorrow, which shew'd that her Love yet remain'd; or else it would not have been such an Affliction to her: . . . She was not at leisure yet, to make Serious Reflections on things past; the Wretchedness of her present State took up all her Thoughts; She could not keep her Eye from what was immediately before her; *Dorante's* Cruelty, and his Poverty were equally Frightful to her; for as the one Scared her with Death, so the other Threatned her with Want. These Dismal Prospects employed her wholly; she could not give her self leave to examine, whether she Hated him or not: But when Time had taken off [a] great part of her Concern, and she was Struck again . . . ; then the Pain made her Angry, and [led her to] think on the Cause, which brought in all the rest; for being now grown acquainted with her Misery, it was not so pressing, as to take up every Moment of her Time; She had more Leisure to call to Mind, and Sedately Review, what was past: She now made use of her Reason, Examin'd the vast extent of her former Love; and, Measuring by that, the prodigious height of his Ingratitude, Built her Hatred on a Solid Foundation. (87–88)

Despite the opportunities afforded by his theme, Mandeville does not seek to titillate his readers with prurient detail or suggestive innuendo. In context, Lucinda's occasionally earthy anatomical references serve comic rather than pornographic ends. Yet there is in *The Virgin Unmask'd* an unusual degree of sexual realism, especially in such passages as those wherein Lucinda (as the table of contents puts it) "relates all the Actions by which she found out that Nature had begun to work upon her Niece":

Sometimes when you thought you was not observ'd, how passionately would you throw yourself backward, and clapping your Legs alternatively over one another, squeeze your Thighs together with all the Strength you had, and in a Quarter of an Hour repeat the same to all the Chairs in the Room? Many Times, *Antonia*, have I seen you sit in that Careless Manner, and half shutting your Eyes, whilst your Head would slowly drop down to one Shoulder, bite on your Lip with so Craving, and so Begging a Look, that I have pitied you my self, and spoke, to make you think on something else: Every Action, and every Limb, betray'd your Desires, your Tongue only excepted; nay, I have often fear'd that that likewise would have been drawn into the Plot, and ask'd for Man as loud as they. (21–22)

Even in an age as relatively unblushing as the early eighteenth century, so graphic and explicit a picture of an adolescent girl's autoeroticism required considerable boldness. Only two years before the appearance of *The Virgin Unmask'd* John Marshall had been prosecuted for publishing *The School of Love*, the indictment specifically condemning the work's overt references to female masturbation techniques.[4]

In his preface to *The Virgin Unmask'd*, Mandeville had remarked: "By leaving the Story of *Leonora* unfinished, you may expect I intend to go on" (x), though of course he never did. We need not be in much doubt, however, as to that story's denouement. We may assume that Lucinda would never have offered the anecdote if its conclusion did not reinforce her contention that even the chastest woman may fall victim to a wily seducer. Indeed, Leonora's ultimate surrender had already been clearly acknowledged when Lucinda introduced her story as "a sad Instance of one, that only for Want of apprehending the Danger, without being ravish'd, was robb'd of her Honour" (183). But, if Mandeville has made the outcome of Leonora's story obvious enough, the didactic intentions of the curious work whose conclusion it furnishes are rather less clear.

II *The "Fair Sex" Debate*

In addressing himself to the topic of the role and status of women, Mandeville was entering into a literary and sociological controversy that flourished very nearly as much in his time as it has in ours. During the latter part of the seventeenth and the earlier part of the eighteenth centuries, participants in the so-called "Fair-Sex" debate argued on such related topics as women's intellectual and moral qualities compared to men's; the appropriate extent and nature of female education; the wife's role in marriage; and so on. Surveying the literature of this debate, Rae Blanchard has divided its contributors into three broad categories—the conservatives, the reformers, and the wits.

The conservatives, supported by tradition, law, and custom, were those who considered women to be morally and mentally inferior to men and hence properly subordinate, both collectively in society and individually in marriage. This is the general view behind such influential works as *The Ladies' Calling* (1671—generally attributed to Richard Allestree), the Marquis of Halifax's *Advice to a Daughter* (1688), and *Instructions for the Education of a Daughter* (1707—a translation by George Hickes of François de Fénelon's *De l'Éducation des Filles*, 1687). In opposition to this view were the reformers, who rejected the idea that women were naturally inferior to men and who advocated an equality of education and legal status between the sexes. Among the more prominent works embodying this view were Mary Astell's *A Serious Proposal to the Ladies* (Part I—1694; Part II—1697), *Some Serious Reflections Upon Marriage* (1703), and Daniel Defoe's proposal on education for women in the *Essay on Projects* (1697).

Somewhere between the conservatives and the reformers fell a less easily defined group—the wits, whose expressed opinions on the subject varied but whose primary emphases were literary rather than hortatory. Some wits denounced women (as does Robert Gould in *Love Given Over*, 1680); others issued gallant, if patronizing celebrations of feminine delicacy (as does Charles de St. Évremond in *Idée da la femme qui ne se trouve point et qui ne se trovera jamais*, 1667); and still others offered "balanced" viewpoints in which lists of alleged female faults are matched by analogous virtues (as does William Walsh in his *Dialogue Concerning Women*, 1691). The degree to which personal conviction entered into the opinions expressed in such works is debatable since their authors were most often speaking through personae and following well-established satiric genres and conventions.[5]

Mandeville's *The Virgin Unmask'd* does not lend itself to simple inclusion in any one of these three categories, although the work shares certain attitudes and qualities with all three. Thus Lucinda, for all her feminism, is conservative in such things as her acceptance of a double sexual standard. Moreover, she readily acknowledges that, "In Reasoning, Women can never cope with Men, they have a Thousand Advantages beyond us.... Women are shallow Creatures; we may boast of Prattling, and be quick at a Jest, or Repartee, but a sound and penetrating Judgment only belongs to Men, as the Masters of Reason and solid Sense" (27–28). However, like the reformers, Lucinda clearly sees women as unjustly oppressed; and she argues vigorously for increased female education and independence. Yet if we try to determine Mandeville's position (as distinct from Lucinda's) in *The Virgin Unmask'd*, we immediately confront the question posed by the writings of the wits: To what extent is it permissible to ascribe to an author personally opinions expressed by fictional characters in an imaginative work?

Both dramatically and quantitatively, *The Virgin Unmask'd* is dominated by Lucinda, who expresses her opinions at length and with very little more than token opposition from her niece. Though in his promised continuation of the work Mandeville may perhaps have planned to introduce a fuller series of counterarguments, Lucinda's assertive case against masculine tyranny over women goes largely unchallenged in the book as we have it. Under the circumstances, many readers might well assume that Lucinda represents Mandeville's own viewpoint, even though Mandeville writes in his preface: "My Design through the whole, is to let young Ladies know whatever is dreadful in Marriage, and this could not be done, but by introducing one that was an Enemy to it. Therefore, tho' *Lucinda* speaks altogether against Matrimony, don't think that I do so too" (ix).

That Mandeville's opinions on marriage, sex, and female modesty are widely divergent from Lucinda's becomes apparent from even a casual survey of his other works. For example, by way of contrast to Lucinda's strong disapproval of Antonia's fashionably low-cut dress, we may consider Mandeville's comment in Remark C of the *Fable of the Bees:* "A Woman is not to be found fault with for going with her Neck bare, if the Custom of the Country allows of it; and when the Mode orders the Stays to be cut very low, a blooming Virgin may, without Fear of rational Censure, shew all the World:

How firm her pouting Breasts, that white as Snow,
On th' ample Chest at mighty distance grow."[6]

Likewise, in the *Enquiry into the Origin of Honour,* Cleomenes (whom Mandeville elsewhere specifically acknowledges as his alter-ego) points out that women who deliberately choose to live out their lives as virgins are of two classes: those who enter nunneries (usually at so young an age that their decision is not really their own) and those (like Lucinda) who are unwilling to put themselves at the mercy of any man. "The Motive [of the latter] is no other, than . . . their Vanity, the undoubted Offspring of Self-liking, a palpable Excess, an extravagant Degree of the Passion, that is able to stifle the loudest Calls of Nature, and with a high Hand triumphs over all other Appetites and Inclinations."[7] Mandeville's customary treatment of sexual subjects (as, for example, in the erotic poems of *Wishes to a Godson* or in the *Modest Defence of Publick Stews)* hardly suggests puritan severity, and it would not be hard to multiply instances to demonstrate how far Lucinda's attitudes are from those of her creator.

Given this discrepancy, we might at first assume that Mandeville's portrait of Lucinda is primarily satirical in intent, but neither her person nor her views are subjected to any overt mockery. Though Mandeville certainly disagrees with a great many of her opinions, he sees to it that they are argued with a skill and conviction which are never directly undercut or ridiculed. Had Mandeville wished to render Lucinda absurd, it would have been easy for him to have presented her in the time-honored role of the frigid old maid, frantically cherishing the virginity she has never been able to dispose of. There are admittedly a few faint traces of such a character in Lucinda—as, for example, in her bitter comment on Antonia's breasts: "See how filthily and boldly they stand pouting out, and bid defiance to your Stays; one would not think that any Thing made of Flesh could be so hard and ugly as they are" (9). But, on the whole, Lucinda is not made comic in any obvious way. There are even a good many instances in which she clearly *is* Mandeville's spokesman who quite seriously enunciates his viewpoint. Thus such things as Lucinda's opinion that the morality of an action can be determined only by its motives (73); her discussion of contemporary political prejudices (Dialogues Seven and Eight); and her recommendation of diet and exercise as a cure for Antonia's moodiness (111) all reflect ideas which Mandeville elsewhere espouses in his own voice.

In *The Virgin Unmask'd*, then, Mandeville presents us with a character of considerable dignity, who—without effective contradiction and displaying much peripheral good sense—skillfully advocates a position that is essentially at odds with Mandeville's own. In the strategy of this complicated stance we may detect certain features which play a large role in Mandeville's later works. Having conceived of Lucinda not merely as opinionated but also as intelligent, sharp-witted, and knowledgeable, Mandeville naturally endowed her with all the polemical talents appropriate to such a woman. In a rhetorical tactic analogous to that so often used by his contemporary, Jonathan Swift, Mandeville employs his fictional creation to argue persuasively, logically, and even compellingly on behalf of what is ultimately a crankish absurdity—the renunciation by women not only of their subordinate status, but of marriage and sex itself.

It is significant that in her rejection of marriage as an institution, Lucinda adopts a position more extreme than that publicly taken by any contemporary writer on feminism, whether conservative, reformer, or wit, all of whom agreed that the real goal of women should be marriage.[8] The reader of *The Virgin Unmask'd* who finds himself (or perhaps more often herself) agreeing with Lucinda's more reasonable contentions—that cunning seducers often callously prey on naive young ladies; that wives are frequently abused or neglected by their husbands; that every marriage is rich in the possibilities of personal tragedy—is finally pulled up short when he discovers how Mandeville has by degrees manipulated him into very nearly assenting to Lucinda's superficially plausible, but psychologically and realistically untenable proposition —namely, that women can best protect themselves from the dangers inherent in sexuality by rejecting it altogether.

Since the obvious arguments against Lucinda's philosophy are either not presented at all or at best are very feebly voiced by Antonia, the reader's impulse is to interpose his own objections, reservations, and refutations; and, as Mandeville well knows, such self-persuasion is by far the most effective sort. In *The Virgin Unmask'd*, as he had already done in *The Grumbling Hive* and was to do more fully yet in *The Fable of the Bees*, Mandeville treats a moral and social question in terms so deliberately uncompromising that the reader must choose between a bleakly unworkable rigorism on the one hand and a human and hence imperfect reality on the other. In this sense, the virgin whose deceptive mask Mandeville has pulled away in this work is not the posturing adolescent Antonia but rather the self-congratulatory Lucinda who has reasoned herself into a life of literal and figurative sterility.

CHAPTER 4

Mandeville as a Physician

W HEN, in the 1690's, Mandeville decided to settle in England, one of his motives may well have been his belief as a specialist in nervous disorders that in no other European country would he be likely to find so plentiful a supply of patients. Throughout much of the seventeenth and eighteenth centuries there is remarkable agreement among foreign observers about the English propensity for melancholia, morbid gloom, and self-destruction. The English, far from issuing denials, ruefully admitted the justice of such allegations. The poets and writers (themselves frequently sufferers) gave ample witness in such works as Robert Burton's *Anatomy of Melancholy* (1621), Lady Winchilsea's *Of the Spleen* (1709), Matthew Green's *The Spleen* (1737), Edward Young's *Night Thoughts* (1742–1746), and Oliver Goldsmith's *Citizen of the World* (1762).[1] Adding weight to the testimony of the poets was the near unanimity of opinion among doctors. In 1682, Dr. Thomas Sydenham, in his *Epistolary Dissertation to Dr. Cole*, asserted that "the hysterical disease" was the commonest chronic ailment in England. His opinion was reiterated in the early eighteenth century by such medical works as Dr. John Purcell's *Treatise of Vapours and Hysterick Fits* (1702), Dr. William Stukeley's *Of the Spleen* (1723), and Sir Richard Blackmore's *Treatise of the Spleen and Vapours: Or Hypochondriacal and Hysterical Affections* (1725). When, in 1733, Dr. George Cheyne called his book on hypochondria *The English Malady*, he was merely underlining what his readers had long ago learned to accept as a melancholy truth.

I Melancholia

As its wide variety of names suggests, the English Malady was among the most protean of diseases, for it embraced a range of mental disturbances broad enough to extend from the simple ennui and imaginary illness of the fashionable lady (so frequently satirized on the stage) to the actual madness of Bedlam's inmates. The symptoms, particularly in severe cases, were almost as various as the patients they attacked. In its milder forms, the disease merely produced a general depression, irritability, and a sense of disquiet; but, as the ailment progressed, it could generate acute anxiety feelings, sometimes accompanied by hallucination and irrational behavior; and more advanced victims might suffer such conflicting symptoms as either lassitude or violent agitation, loss of appetite or morbid gluttony, torpor or convulsions, or (in some especially unfortunate cases) all these afflictions in turn. Clearly, so polymorphous a disease did not lend itself to easy treatment; and, though doctors were agreed as to the prevalence of the malady, they varied widely in their theories about its origin and cure.

The different names which were applied to the disease reflect something of its history and the prevailing ideas concerning its nature. From Greek medicine came the term "melancholia," which derives from the ancient belief that all illness results from an imbalance of the four bodily "humours," in this case an excess of noxious black choler. Also from the Greeks came the distinction between "melancholia" and "hysteria" (from the Greek word for womb) which, since it is caused by a displacement of the uterus, was considered peculiar to women. During the Middle Ages and Renaissance in England these terms were commonly used to cover such mental aberrations as were not ascribable to demonic possession.

In the seventeenth century, however, fashion and new medical theories produced a series of additional names. In the reign of James I the word "spleen," referring to the organ which many doctors believed responsible for producing black choler, began to be used to describe the malady itself. Less specific was the term "hypochondria," which suggested only that the disease originated somewhere in the *hypochondrium*—that portion of the body cavity below the breastbone. Since the "humours" which caused the disease had to assume vaporous form before they could ascend the hollow nerves and reach the brain, the term "vapours" gained favor in the latter part of the century. There was some attempt by medical writers (Mandeville among them) to limit the use of these terms to different manifestations and varieties of mental illness, but in general practice they came to be used almost interchangeably. Thus, the term "hysteria" began to lose its exclusively feminine character after Dr. Sydenham explained it as simply another species of melancholia. Likewise, "vapours," also originally used with reference only to women, soon lost its sexual qualification and became general.

To explain the English vulnerability to melancholia, medical opinion most often cited climate and diet, since it was felt that chilly, rainy, foggy weather, combined with a national penchant for heavy foods (particularly beef), tended to stimulate those atrabilious humours which in excess produced the "hyp." Though no one was immune, the leisure classes suffered a special susceptability; and, among these, women (because of their delicate natures) and scholars (because of their sedentary lives and mental exertions) furnished the majority of victims. In choosing the wealthy, bookish Misomedon, his high-spirited wife, and their sensitive daughter to serve as his case histories in his *Treatise of the Hypochondriack and Hysterick Passions* (1711), Mandeville offers portraits of persons whose social class and personal temperaments qualify them as representative patients.

II *The Characters*

Representative though they may be, the *hypochondraici* who figure in Mandeville's *Treatise* emerge as something more than the faceless clinical types found in most medical works. The dialogue form, with its conversational informality and its personal interplay, creates opportunities for characterization akin to those of the drama. To exploit these opportunities Mandeville is at some pains to individualize his more important *dramatis personae* and to shape his presentation so as not to violate the personalities he has given them. In his preface, after anticipating that apothecaries may be displeased by some of the unflattering remarks about them in the text, Mandeville somewhat disingenuously denies any intent to insult by asking that apothecaries "consider, how profess'd an Enemy to Physick, and over fond of University-learning *Misomedon* (who is the Man that exclaims against them) is represented to be throughout the Book." As Mandeville explains, "without spoiling his Character I could not have made him speak otherwise than he does."[2] The same concern for consistency of characterization is repeated later in the preface, where Mandeville answers critics who might complain of the heavy use of technical terms and quotations in learned languages:

In reply to [such critics], I shall tell them, that it was Decency, that forc'd me to what they complain of: And that considering, who the Persons are, that compose the Dialogue, to observe the Rules of it, I could not let *Misomedon* talk otherwise, than a Man of Learning, that had made Physick his particular Study, would to a Physician whom he consults about his Distemper. It would be ridiculous to hear two Men discoursing together, Translate to one another, what both are supposed to understand. (ix)

Despite the learned terms and Latin quotations, Mandeville makes it clear that his *Treatise* is intended for patients rather than for his fellow doctors. Aware that the usual medical text, with its endless enumeration of diagnostic signs and varieties of treatment, "must be very tiresome and disagreeable to People that seek relief in a Distemper of which Impatience is one of the surest Symptoms, I resolv'd to deviate from the usual method, and make what I had to say as palatable as I could..." (viii). To achieve this palatability Mandeville offers his readers not only a conversational format and characters with whom they can identify, but a variety of anecdotal digressions on such topics as the training of doctors, the signs by which one may detect a quack, the greed and incompetence of some apothecaries, and the hauteur and callousness of some physicians. There is even an attempt to create a kind of dramatic suspense. Thus, Mandeville does not reveal his own explanation of the causes of hypochondriac and hysteric passions until the book is half over, and his prescribed remedies are not disclosed until very near its conclusion.

The two principal characters who figure in the dialogue are Misomedon, a long-time sufferer from the "hyp," and Philopirio, the physician he has sent for. The latter is of particular interest, since Mandeville acknowledges in his preface that, "In these Dialogues, I have done the same as *Seneca* did in his *Octavia*, and brought my self upon the Stage; with this difference, that he kept his own Name, and I changed mine for that of *Philopirio*, a Lover of Experience, which I shall always profess to be: Wherefore I desire my Reader to take whatever is spoke by the Person I named last, as said by my self" (xi).

Confirming the closeness of the identification are the details of his background and education which Philopirio volunteers during the course of the dialogue. Like Mandeville, he is of Dutch birth, a graduate in medicine of Leyden, and the son of a doctor who also specialized in hypochondria. Such congruences of biographical detail make it clear that Mandeville intends Philopirio not only as a spokesman for his creator's medical opinions but as a self-portrait whose personality and manner the reader is tacitly invited to accept as Mandeville's own.

As we might gather from his name, Philopirio is a man who distrusts those theories and explanations of disease which are based upon abstract speculation rather than on the accumulated data of direct observation. Though learning divorced from practical knowledge wins his scorn, he recognizes the importance of formal study as an essential requirement in the training of a doctor, and he himself is thoroughly versed in medical literature. He bears his learning lightly, but he is never at a loss when the erudite Misomedon (who has made a special study of his disease) cites obscure works and scholarly dissertations. Nor is Philopirio's knowledge limited to professional matters: he is well-grounded in Classical literature, as well as modern European languages; and, when Misomedon quotes a line from Horace or Virgil, Philopirio can gracefully respond by quoting the next. In manner he is polite and obliging, but without obsequiousness to the somewhat overbearing Misomedon.

Philopirio shows his moral rectitude and professional integrity in such things as his refusal to promise cures he cannot deliver and his practice of mixing his own drugs in order to insure purity of ingredients and to save his patients from the exorbitant fees charged by apothecaries. Mandeville is aware, of course, that in displaying his alter-ego in such flattering terms he lays himself open to the charge of self-praise, but it is a risk he is willing to take, for as he says in his preface (prior to informing readers who may wish to consult him that he can be reached through his bookseller): "If a Regular Physician writing of a Distemper, the Cure of which he particularly professes, after a manner never attempted yet, be a *Quack*, because besides his Design of being instructive and doing Good to others, he has likewise an aim of making himself more known by it than he was before, then I am one" (xiii).

Misomedon (whose name may be rendered as "hater of restraint") is pictured as a man given to immoderate enthusiasms and dislikes. His love of study has made him a pedant who enjoys flaunting his knowledge and who has strong opinions which he expresses outspokenly and usually at great length. His manner with Philopirio (at least initially) is brusque and skeptical, though he does not exercise upon Philopirio the sarcasm which is his favorite mode toward the various doctors under whose treatment he has previously suffered. He is a wealthy man, and once Philopirio has impressed him, he is generous with both his compliments and his money. Though he bitterly resents being patronized, particularly by doctors, he is himself condescendingly ironical toward his wife (and fellow hypochondriac) Polytheca, who appears briefly in the third dialogue. She, like her husband, has strong opinions; but, unlike him, she is not willing to be reasoned out of them. She has come to rely heavily upon the impressively packaged drugs with which shrewd apothecaries supply her; hence, the name "Polytheca," which may be translated as "one with many containers"—pillboxes. So firm is her faith in drugs that she is equally impervious to her husband's taunts and Philopirio's advice on behalf of her daughter, who does not appear but whose case history is given in some detail.

III *The* Treatise

The first dialogue takes place in the study of Misomedon, who greets Philopirio with the words: "I have sent for you, Doctor, to consult you about a Distemper of which I am very well assured, I shall never be Cured" (1). After specifying that Philopirio should hear him out "without interrupting," Misomedon begins a detailed history of his illness. As a youth studying law in London, Misomedon inherited an estate worth three hundred pounds a year; he quit his studies and traveled abroad, living in such reckless dissipation that in three years he had squandered all his money. He was saved from physical and financial ruin by his timely marriage to Polytheca, whose fortune restored his wealth and whose charms led him to abandon his profligacy. But after some six years of happy domesticity ("Love and Pastime was all our Employment, from Morning till Night"—4), his wife's money ran out, and Misomedon once again faced bankruptcy. Before matters became desperate, however, a distant relative propitiously died, leaving Misomedon "a Thousand a Year in Land, and a good Estate in Money" (4–5). Financially secure at last, Misomedon settled down and devoted himself to the intense study of Classical literature, which had been a long-deferred passion of his.

Through all the vagaries of his youth Misomedon's health had been excellent, but at thirty-seven the first symptoms of his illness began. Initially these were nothing more than mild digestive disorders. They grew progressively worse, however, as he sought treatment from various doctors, whose remedies, when they helped at all, merely produced a temporary relief followed by attacks of redoubled severity. With understandable bitterness (and in great detail), Misomedon describes all the different medicines he took and how little they alleviated the stomach aches, convulsions, swellings, dizziness, and back pains which had turned him into an invalid by his forties. In self-defense, he took up the study of physic, reading extensively in Greek, Latin, and modern medical works. Meanwhile, his disease, unchecked, advanced beyond the physical into full-fledged hypochondria:

When the Disease was got up into my Head, even tho' the Pain was tolerable, I always was troubled with severe watchings, and lay tossing whole Nights without closing my Eyes, and if I did, I either Dream'd of being Robb'd, of Murder, or else of falling from a Precipice, Drowning, or that I was hang'd. . . .

The sleeps I had were ever disturb'd and wearied instead of reviving me; I generally wak'd out of 'em in a fright, and often in cold Sweats. When these disorders in *ipsa arce, & sede animae*, had lasted for some time, strange roving thoughts would slide through my Brain, and wild as well as ridiculous Fancies stole upon me, and for a while employ'd my Imagination. I had often unaccountable apprehensions of things, which tho' one moment I thought 'em absurd, I could hardly conquer the next with all my strength of Reason. (23–24)

Plagued by these latter symptoms for the past twelve years (especially in the winter), Misomedon at fifty-one has become a "Crazy Valetudinarian," convinced that "the Art of Physick is no more to be depended upon than that of Astrology, and that even the Learned Professors of the first have rendred themselves neither less ridiculous or more beneficial to the Publick than the Ignorant Pretenders to the latter" (30).

In response to this account Philopirio defends the nobility of medicine as an art, but he agrees that a good many doctors are either too theoretical, too lazy, or too avaricious to live up to their primary obligations as healers. Mandeville's contempt for the fashionable physician is vividly expressed in Philopirio's long speech describing the means by which professional success is customarily obtained:

Where shall you find a Physician now a-days, that makes that stay with his Patients, which it is plain, the Ancients must have done to make the noble Prognosticks we have from them. But this would not only be too laborious, but a tedious way of getting Money; self-interest now gives better lessons to young Physicians. . . . rather than that you should spend your Time before the squallid Beds of poor Patients, and bear with the unsavory smells of a crouded Hospital, shew your self a Scholar, write a Poem, either a good one, or a large one; Compose a *Latin* Oration, or do but Translate something out of that Language with your Name to it. If you can do none of all these, Marry into a good Family, and your Relations will help you into Practice: Or else cringe and make your court to half a dozen noted Apothecaries, promise 'em to prescribe loads of Physick. . . . Otherwise be a rigid Party-Man, it is all one, *Whig* or *Tory,* so you are but violent enough of either side; or if you can Chat, and be a good Companion, you may Drink your self into Practice; but if you are too dull for what I have hitherto named, and in reality good for nothing, you must say little and be civil to all the World, keep a set of Coffee-Houses, observe your certain Hours, and take care you are often sent for, where you are, and ask'd for where you are not. . . . (35–37)

Since it is not to be expected that one man could ever master all types of illness, says Philopirio, each serious doctor should select a specialty and become expert in it. Like his father before him, Philopirio has made the hypochondriac and hysteric passions his particular study. He explains that he subscribes fully to none of the current theories of hypochondria, finding all of them too abstract and speculative. Proper understanding of a disease comes only from close and extended observation of many patients, however disagreeable or difficult such observations may be. One of his own motives in choosing hypochondria as his specialty, Philopirio confesses, was its character as "a Chronick Disease, where the attendance should be neither so constant, nor so unpleasant" (56) as would be the case with many other maladies. Misomedon declares himself well-pleased with the honesty of Philopirio's manner and the common sense of his sentiments, and the two men agree to meet again the next day for a full explication of Philopirio's as yet unspecified ideas about hypochondria.

The first indication as to the nature of Philopirio's theory comes early in the second dialogue, when (after expressing gratitude for yesterday's generous fee) he informs Misomedon that "by what I know from Observation, it is demonstrable to me, that the cause of Hypochondriack and Histerick Diseases is in the Stomach" (82). Others, he admits, have pointed to the same general source; but he differs sharply from them in his view of the actual process by which the illness is generated. Before elaborating on his thesis, Philopirio (in response to Misomedon's urging) undertakes to specify his objections to those theories which place the seat of the trouble in such places as the spleen, the brain, or the pancreas. What follows is a lengthy consideration in turn of each of the prominent schools of opinion concerning the origins and nature of hypochondria. With Misomedon occasionally interspersing counterarguments, Philopirio systematically points out the weaknesses which have led him to reject all or part of each rival hypothesis.

As we might expect, Philopirio's fundamental complaint in every case boils down to a distrust of large assertions unsupported by clinical evidence. It is the habit of too many, he says, to put forth as certainty that which is either mostly speculative or, in some cases, actually contrary to observable fact. Typical is his scorn for those who pretend to circumstantial knowledge of physiological processes whose real natures are as yet undetermined:

We are altogether in the Dark, as to the real use the Liver, the Milt, and Pancreas are of to our Bodies; nay, wholly ignorant of their several Offices otherwise than that they are *Organa Colatoria*, through which something is strain'd, and all that has been said of them besides, by the most Sagacious Men has been nothing but Conjectures, in which the best Anatomists could yet never agree: If we consider, with how little certainty we can speak of Organs so Conspicuous, such gross and large *Viscera*, is it not amazing to see some Men made of no other Mold, nor assisted with more helps in Anatomy than you or I, suppose themselves... well acquainted with things invisible and almost incomprehensible... ? (103–04)

Though Philopirio's refutation of other physicians's theories is trenchant and closely reasoned, it is rather dull reading, involving as it does a great many technical terms and frequent quotation from Latin treatises. Even so concerned an auditor as Misomedon finds the going heavy, and at one point he peevishly remarks: "As I brought you upon talking of *Hypotheses*, I suppose against your Inclination, so I see, you are resolv'd to fit me for it, and design to tire me with them before you give over" (116). Tedious or not, Philopirio's discussion of his predecessors's errors is a necessary preliminary to the presentation of his own ideas, the explication of which takes up the last portion of the second dialogue. With a wealth of example and illustration drawn from his observation of patients, Philopirio affirms his conviction that hypochondria ultimately stems from disorder of the digestive juices.

The stomach, as Philopirio explains, is lined with thousands of hollow nerve endings through which it receives the "Animal Spirits" that form an essential ingredient of the "Stomachick Ferment" or digestive juices. These animal spirits are composed of both fine and gross particles, of which a delicate balance is required for good digestion. The fine particles, however, are also used by the brain, which consumes them in the process of thought. Hence, any unusual mental expenditure, whether through study or anxiety, will draw the fine particles away from the stomach and thus produce digestive disorders. By the same token, the grosser animal spirits, besides their intestinal function, are used by the body in its muscular movements; and, when insufficiently so employed, these gross particles will accumulate to excess in the stomach, eventually turning "sour" and causing trouble. As a result, the scholar and the sensitive woman, both of whom are characterized by over-active minds and under-active bodies, are particularly prone to dyspepsia. In mild cases, the disease may progress no further, but when the improper "Volatilization of the Stomachick Ferment" becomes acute, the entire body will be affected in a variety of unpleasant ways. Eventually the imbalance of animal spirits in the brain will produce such symptoms as the depression, terror, hallucinations, and irritability of the confirmed hypochondriac. Misomedon's case has been especially severe because he not only leads a sedentary life of unusual mental exertion, but in his youth—first as a rake and then as a loving husband—he had been sexually immoderate; and, as Philopirio points out, few things are so disruptive of the animal spirits as an "Excess of *Venery*."

Such—in simplified form and without the detailed account of specific symptoms and variations—is Philopirio's explanation of hypochondria. Throughout Philopirio's presentation, Misomedon, who acts as an *adversarius*, raises objections and demands clarifications. Almost against his will, however, he gradually finds himself won over, finally paying Philopirio a compliment all the more gratifying because of the obvious reluctance with which it is issued:

It is very strange, and sure something belonging to my Distemper, that whatever resolution I take up against Physick and Physicians, I should always hearken to the last comer. It is without doubt the ardent desire we have for our welfare, that in spite of our Reason makes us so fond of believing: I find my self again perswaded, and tho' I have often fancy'd the same in vain, yet now methinks I am convinced of the real Cause, not only of the Crudities and their grievous Effects, but likewise all the innumerable other Symptoms, that have ever disturb'd me. (147–48)

The last traces of Misomedon's doubt disappear when Philopirio frankly tells him that in so confirmed a case as his a complete cure beyond danger of relapse is not to be expected, though with proper care the disease can be contained. So impressed is Misomedon that, without even waiting to hear the prescribed treatment, he announces that he will comply with whatever Philopirio commends. Misomedon asks Philopirio to return the next day, though now, significantly, their relationship has become a social, as well as professional, one since the invitation is to dinner.

After dinner the next day, Misomedon questions Philopirio

about why women, who so seldom sin in the direction of mental
exertion, should be particularly susceptible to hypochondria.
Philopirio points out that women of the more delicate sort
can ill-afford the expenditure involved in *any* exhaustion of
the brain: "One Hours intense Thinking wastes the Spirits
more in a Woman, than six in a Man" (177). In any case,
hypochondria in women frequently derives from an insuf-
ficient generation of animal spirits, rather than from their
depletion, as with men. Women also often "pauperize" the
blood (where the animal spirits originate) by faulty diet, and
the condition is worsened by the periodic blood loss from
menstruation. When to these conditions an "idle" life is added,
hypochondria—or hysteria, as Philopirio still prefers to call
the disease in females—is all but inevitable. Satisfied with
this answer, Misomedon next produces the sizeable collection
of prescriptions he has accumulated over the years, and
Philopirio offers comments (mostly critical) on their composition and efficacy. He himself, Philopirio explains, is very spar-
ing of chemical medication, preferring more natural treatments.

The two men are then joined by Misomedon's wife,
Polytheca, who opens by saying: "You Gentlemen of Learning
make use of very comprehensive Expressions; the word *Hysterick* must be of a prodigious Latitude to signifie so many
different Evils, unless you mean by it a Disease, that like
the Sin of Ingratitude includes all the rest" (196). Her own
symptoms, she explains, are various enough to include
headaches, cholic, fainting spells, back pains, "trembling" of
the heart, feelings of "unaccountable sadness," and fits of
crying. Among the bitterest aspects of her affliction is the lack
of sympathy she encounters from those who consider her illness imaginary and designed simply to attract attention:

I never dare speak of Vapours, the very name is become a Joke,
and the general notion the Men have of them, is, that they are a
malicious mood, and contriv'd Sullenness of Willful, Extravagant and
Imperious Women, when they are denied, or thwarted in their
unreasonable desires; nay, even Physicians, because they cannot
Cure them, are forc'd to ridicule them in their own Defence, and
a Woman, that is really troubled with Vapours, is pitied by none,
but their unhappy fellow Sufferers, that labour under the same Affliction. (199)

After trying many physicians whose promised cures proved illusory, Polytheca has placed her faith in apothecaries from whom she buys an endless variety of expensive drugs. Despite her husband's ridicule and Philopirio's assurances that such drugs are at best merely palliative, Polytheca is adamant in refusing to change her opinions. She wishes, however, to hear Philopirio's recommendations in the case of her seventeen-year-old daughter who is likewise afflicted. This unfortunate girl not only suffers from all the symptoms that her mother endures, but has had in addition convulsive fits on a monthly schedule since she was eleven. After hearing all the details, Philopirio assures Polytheca that, since the girl is young and the disease (despite its dramatic symptoms) has no firm hold, he can promise complete cure. To this end he prescribes a month of rigorous exercise with no medication at all.

To this advice—Philopirio's first explicit advocacy of a program of treatment—Polytheca and Misomedon react with shock and delight, respectively. Misomedon's approval is based largely on his long-standing contempt for apothecaries and their nostrums. Continuing what is obviously an old subject of debate between them, Misomedon turns to Polytheca and begins an extended denunciation of apothecaries as grasping and ignorant—the remarks which Mandeville (in the quotation from the preface, cited above) had specified were not to be taken as reflecting his own opinion. Indignant apothecaries, however, might be excused for being skeptical since Misomedon's attack has a fullness of detail and a vehemence of assertion that carry a good deal more conviction than does the handful of feeble counterarguments. Aside from Polytheca's few and easily demolished remarks in defense of apothecaries, Misomedon's monologue is interrupted only by an occasional judicious objection of Philopirio's—as when he comments that an intelligent and thoroughly trained apothecary might well be superior to an inexperienced and stupid physician. Misomedon gladly cedes the point, merely observing that such apothecaries are nowhere to be found.

At length, Polytheca, displaying both her disease and her feminine incapacity for sustained argument, abruptly announces:

Oh the Tormenting and Throbbing Pain I feel in my Head! This

Minute my Brains are a boiling, and if there was half a Dozen of Trunk-makers at work under my Skull, I don't think I could be sensible of more Noise and Beating than I am. I can stay no longer. What directions you leave with my Husband, or else in Writing, my Daughter shall punctually observe, I beg your pardon *Philopirio,* for my rudeness, but I am forc'd to withdraw. (233)

After gently chiding Misomedon for having so upset his wife, Philopirio explains more fully that sort of exercise he prescribes for the daughter. Each morning before breakfast she should "be swung for half an Hour," either in a seat suspended by a rope or by some other convenient method. Following a breakfast of bland but nutritious foods, she should first ride horseback for two hours and then be vigorously massaged "till her Skin looks red, and her Flesh glows all over"—the entire program to be repeated in the afternoon. If followed for a month, such a regimen will help to replenish her inadequate supply of fine animal spirits and to eliminate her excess of the gross variety. How she responds, says Philopirio, will indicate whether other measures—such as bleeding, cupping, or baths—are advisable; but he is confident that exercise and careful diet will do wonders.

For Misomedon, Philopirio likewise recommends careful diet (nourishing, easily digestible foods—no supper at all) and physical exercise (no swinging, but much horseback riding). In addition, Misomedon must take frequent baths, cleanse his stomach as required with vomits, and build up his vigor with strengthening medicines. Above all, he is to avoid tiring his mind with either study or domestic cares. If he will do all these things, says Philopirio, "I dare promise you that in a little time you shall see your self chang'd into another Man." Well-pleased by so favorable a prognosis, Misomedon agrees to do as directed, promising Philopirio generous payment if his predictions come true. When Misomedon asks whether the same prescription applies to all hypochondriacs, Philopirio replies that different patients require different specifics, but that restricted diet, physical exercise, and avoidance of mental strain are basic ingredients of any cure. Then, after additional expressions of confidence by Misomedon and an exchange of compliments in Latin, the *Treatise* concludes.

IV *Mandeville as a Proto-Psychiatrist*

Clearly, it would be hard today to sustain any large claims for Mandeville's *Treatise of the Hypochondriack and Hysterick Passions* as a basic contribution to an understanding of the complex sicknesses whose causes and cures it professes to explain. Though Mandeville shows a solid knowledge of contemporary medicine, the advent of psychiatry, as well as immense advances in knowledge of physiology, have inevitably rendered much of his *Treatise* quaintly obsolete. It would be palpably unfair to criticize Mandeville for failing to elucidate maladies whose principles are still in dispute, but even in its own day, Philopirio's account of the genesis of hypochondria must have seemed something of an anticlimax. That account comes only after an attack on all rival theories as speculations which try to pass off ingenious guesswork as if it were incontrovertible fact. Philopirio's explanation of the fine and gross particles in the animal spirits and how they operate is internally consistent and, given the state of medical knowledge in 1711, was no doubt quite plausible; but, for all its claims of clinical support, as a thesis it is scarcely less conjectural and inventive than the theories it seeks to replace.

Yet, if Mandeville's understanding of the origins and nature of nervous disorders is, through no fault of his own, inadequate, there is much to be said for the general course of therapy he advocates. Not only does he deserve praise for his strictures against the usually worthless and sometimes murderous concoctions favored by so many contemporary physicians and apothecaries, but his positive recommendations are, for the most part, eminently sensible. The benefits which the nervously afflicted might hope to gain from moderate diet, healthy exercise, and the avoidance of mental exhaustion seem a good deal more self-evident today than they did in Mandeville's time. Two generations later, so shrewd an observer as Samuel Johnson (who, like Misomedon, had read widely in the literature of his malady) praised the usefulness of Mandeville's *Treatise*,[3] and the practical advice Johnson offered to his fellow-sufferer Boswell echoed many of Philopirio's recommendations.

Mandeville's importance in British medical history, however, is based not so much upon the tangible treatments he prescribed as upon his noteworthy anticipation of elementary psychiatric technique. Throughout the *Treatise* Mandeville demonstrates a steady awareness, remarkable in his time, of the therapeutic value of encouraging patients to express their anxieties fully. It will be recalled that one of Misomedon's complaints against the physicians he had consulted earlier was that none of them was willing to hear him out. The twenty-eight page monologue in which Misomedon gives the history of his disease is interrupted only once, and that is when Philopirio comments: "Your Story is so diverting, that I take abundance of delight in it, and your Ingenious way of telling it, gives me a greater insight into your Distemper, than you imagine" (18). The happy effect of a sympathetic listener upon Misomedon is apparent almost immediately. After he has unburdened himself—and long before Philopirio has offered any diagnosis or advice—Misomedon remarks:

You and I must be better acquainted, *Philopirio;* if your Medicines do me no good, I am sure your Company will: One thing above the rest I admire in you, and that's your Patience, which must be unaffected, because you can be gay in the exercise of it. You can't imagine, how a pertinent lively discourse, or any thing that is sprightly revives my Spirits. I don't know, what it is that makes me so, whether it be our talking together, the Serenity of the Air, or both; but I enjoy abundance of Pleasure, and this moment, methinks, I am as well, as ever I was in my Life. (41)

Throughout the *Treatise* Philopirio makes every effort to draw his patient out, even on the most trivial and tangential matters; and Mandeville's choice of the dialogue form was in all likelihood partially based upon its suitability for illustrating such a process. As a modern historian of British psychiatry says of Mandeville's *Treatise*, "The treatment advocated was in the main psycho-therapeutic—the dialogues between physician and patient may even be regarded as very early 'recorded interviews.' The patients were allowed to ventilate their ideas freely, and to express their hostility to the doctor, a remarkable situation for the early eighteenth century."[4]

Mandeville is also ahead of his time in the concern he shows for the ill effects suffered by the families of the mentally disturbed. Because it was still widely believed that hysteria in young women was caused by a displacement of the womb, doctors frequently prescribed marriage as a necessary part of the cure. Misomedon, anxious over his daughter, at one point asks about the advisability of such a step; and in his reply Philopirio expresses strong disapproval, explaining that "in the first place it may fail, and then there are two People made unhappy instead of one; Secondly it may but half Cure the Woman, who lingring under the remainder of her Disease, may have half a dozen Children, that shall all inherit it" (238). In *Hysteria: The History of a Disease*, Ilza Veith (after quoting Philopirio's statement) comments: "This brief answer is replete with new thought. Countless physicians had recommended such marriages, but none before had expressed an interest in the result of a marriage of a hysterical patient or in the fate of her spouse. The fact that marriage might fail to be a cure, that the children might be affected, and that unhappiness might be multiplied had never before been the concern of physicians."[5]

In the preface to the *Treatise of the Hypochondriack and Hysterick Passions* (as cited above), Mandeville acknowledged that one of his motives in publishing the book was that through it he hoped to make himself better known as a physician. The subsequent publication history of the work suggests that he achieved a distinct, if limited, success in this ambition. After its original appearance in 1711, the *Treatise* was reissued unchanged in 1715, and it appeared twice again in editions of 1730, this time in a somewhat enlarged version. When Mandeville died in 1733, the *Treatise* was well-known enough to qualify as the only book of his, aside from *The Fable of the Bees*, to be mentioned by name in the brief obituary notice that ran in *Berington's Evening Post* and *Applebee's Original Weekly Journal*. The *Treatise* continued to find at least a few appreciative readers (such as Johnson) later in the century, though the medical profession—partly influenced perhaps by Mandeville's extramedical notoriety—was for the most part to reject both his theories and, with considerably less justification, his example as a proto-psychiatrist.

CHAPTER 5

Free Thoughts on Religion

THE early eighteenth century has so often been characterized as an age in which religious belief languished in the face of growing skepticism and rationalism that we sometimes overlook how passionately and extensively the Augustans debated matters of faith. As Roland Stromberg has observed, "the years between 1690 and 1740 were in fact years of crisis in the religious foundations of Western civilization. They were years not so much of languid doubt as of critical tension."[1] The doctrinal animosities which had produced so much bloodshed and persecution in the preceding century now found their readiest expression in violent polemics rather than in violent acts, and the resultant corpus of religious disputation was enormous.

Involved in such controversy were much more than abstruse points of theology, for in an age in which religion and politics were inextricably bound together, there were few areas of national life untouched by sectarian concerns. Though Mandeville's ideas on religion run throughout his works—most notably in *The Fable of the Bees*—his satiric manner often creates a protective ambiguity. Of special interest, therefore, is the *Free Thoughts on Religion, the Church, and National Happiness* (1720) in which Mandeville undertakes *"with Plainness and Sincerity, without Fiction or Enthusiasm,"*[2] to enunciate his views on the central questions of religion and religious politics so furiously argued by his contemporaries.

With the expulsion of James II in 1688, the Church of England had been strengthened and reaffirmed in its position as the official state religion; but, by the early eighteenth century, the brief church unity which had followed the Glorious Revolution had begun to give way to an increasing polarization of opinion concerning the dimensions, directions, and comparative urgency of outside threats to Anglican supremacy.

To the politically and theologically conservative High Churchmen, perhaps the greatest cause for alarm was the collective challenge posed by such Protestant splinter groups as the Baptists, the Presbyterians, the Quakers, and the dozens of lesser dissenting sects. Despite numerous laws which in theory excluded non-Anglicans from all civic and most economic power, the Dissenters as a group had continued to flourish; and High Churchmen—bitterly recalling the Puritan Commonwealth and anxious above all to prevent a recurrence—firmly pressed for a course of stricter measures designed to enforce doctrinal orthodoxy and, if possible, to extirpate all schism.

Low Church Anglicans, on the other hand, found less to fear from Dissenters than from the prospect of a Roman Catholic resurgence in Britain. As a tiny, harrassed, and largely powerless minority of the population, the English Catholics would have seemed a negligible menace had it not been for the exiled Pretender, whose claim to the throne had been endorsed by the French monarch and whose return at the head of an invading army appeared to many to be an imminent threat. Given the circumstances, the Low Church Latitudinarians were willing to tolerate Dissenters—even to welcome them as valuable allies in the doctrinal and political struggle against Catholicism and its Jacobite sympathizers among High Church conservatives.

It was not sectarianism alone, however, that aroused religious anxieties in the early eighteenth century. A much more profound threat, all the more disquieting because it was so ill-defined, was the growth of rationalism, often within the ranks of the Church itself. Partly in reaction to the chaotic "enthusiasm" of the Puritans and partly as a result of the prestige of the new science, there were widespread efforts after the Restoration to subject Christianity to a purely rational interpretation. Initially, as with John Locke and Isaac Newton, such efforts were meant to bolster belief by demonstrating how perfectly reason came to the support of faith. As later writers discovered, however, the same rational approach could be applied to the rejection of the very mysteries which for the orthodox were the bedrock of religion itself. To alarmed traditionalists it seemed both presumptuous and heretical to promulgate a Christianity totally accessible to human understanding, and the term "deist"—loosely applied to all those who sought to minimize the miraculous in religion—most often appears in the polemics of the time as a near equivalent for "atheist."

It is into this context, in which all factions felt beleaguered and in which any stand could be relied upon to provoke heated denunciation from some quarter, that Mandeville stepped forward with his *Free Thoughts on Religion, the Church, and National Happiness*. Something of the violence with which contemporary religious controversy was conducted is suggested by the way Mandeville, in his preface, describes the verbal abuse and worse which he expects his work to elicit:

> I well know the common Fate of Moderation; it neither procures you Friends, nor appeases your Enemies, and fixes a Man as a Mark to the two Factions, that place themselves in the opposite Extream: But I have still worse to fear, considering the bold Truths I have spoke; and many will wonder at my Temerity, and ask, Who is it; Has he a great Estate? What Calling, or Employment does he follow? Does he ever intend to thrive, or indeed to live? Is he Pistol proof, and does he imagine, there are no Daggers, nor no Poyson in the World? (xvii)

There is, of course, a sizeable element of bravado in Mandeville's pose: physical attack by outraged readers, though by no means unheard of, was nevertheless a relatively remote occupational hazard for the controversial pamphleteer. Self-dramatics aside, however, it remains true that it took no little courage on Mandeville's part to issue his book with so little effort to preserve his anonymity. Few interested readers can have been long uncertain as to the identity of an author who signs his title-page "By B.M.," and who twice quotes extensively from *The Fable of the Bees* in elaboration of his views. (342, 356)

Though Mandeville's position in the *Free Thoughts* is essentially nonsectarian, in several important respects his stand is analogous to that of an unusually liberal Low Church Anglican. It is true that much of what he says and more of what he implies might rouse the ire of even the least dogmatic Latitudinarian, but in general terms his approach is that of a Church of England communicant, albeit one who is highly skeptical of some of his church's most cherished pretensions.

He does not question the basic truths of Christianity, but in the interests of "Peace and Charity" he urges his more zealous coreligionists to moderate their persecuting impulses, most particularly toward the Dissenters. This is not to say that he considers the Dissenters anything less than misguided fanatics, but he is unwilling to endorse a policy of suppression which, in his opinion, would serve as a religious stalking horse for the political tyranny that, he feels, always follows when clergymen are given too much power.

Despite the perennial complaint that irreligion is on the increase, genuine atheism, says Mandeville, is extremely rare. Most Englishmen sincerely accept the Christian faith in one form or another, though very few find it possible to conform to the moral requirements of their religion. The sins which men commit spring not so much from indifference to religion as from the inability of most people to subdue their appetites and passions. Even those who lead lives of seeming rectitude frequently do so from ignoble motives of vanity or fear, for "there is a vast Difference between not committing an Immorality from a Principle of Pride and Prudence, and the avoiding of Sin for the Love of GOD" (10). Thus, Mandeville (as in *The Fable of the Bees*) takes the most ascetic view of morality, refusing to accept as good any behavior, however virtuous in appearance or result, that partakes at all of self-love. From this rigorous position Mandeville considers the various evasions by which men pretend to fulfill the obligations of a religion whose real demands they are unwilling to face.

The outward signs of devotion are those most easily complied with, and accordingly there are many whose religion consists almost exclusively of the careful observation of rites and ceremonies. Under Roman Catholicism, says Mandeville, the proliferation of rituals and sacraments became an important means by which priests could increase their own power while convincing their parishioners that the remission of sins required little more than an outlay of money and a few symbolic prayers. The Reformation has done away with many such practices, but the more extreme Dissenters would like to abolish *all* rites except those few with clear biblical authority. Mandeville feels that such action would be excessive; for, although most Christian ceremonies are of purely human invention, they cannot be called pernicious unless they are offered as a substitute for, rather than as an encouragement to, genuine faith.

In any case, the elimination of religious ceremonies can never change the human propensity for self-deception, as becomes clear when one considers how such things as scrupulously regular church attendance have a way of becoming the Protestant equivalents of the ritual observances by which Catholics evade the demands of real piety. Under the circumstances, wisdom suggests a policy in which idolatrous rituals are forbidden, harmless ones tolerated, and none but the most sacred ones insisted upon. To be dogmatical about matters so peripheral to true religion is dangerous as well as foolish, for such stubbornness is necessarily destructive of the religious unity which should always be the goal of a national church:

Thus I would speak to those of our own Church, and conclude with this Admonition: If the Dissenters are deluded, let us shew that we are the wisest. Is the continuance of their Separation obstinacy in them, let us avoid the same Imputation, by not urging the Dispute any further. If to err belongs to humane Frailty, let us bear with their Errors, and for the future resolve to treat them with Humanity; and begin with three Things that ought to be· easy to a Christian: Let us forbear calling Names, ascribing Sentiments to them, which they utterly disown, and laying to the Charge of any of them, what they have not been personally guilty of themselves. (56–57)

In all Christianity there is scarcely a sect or denomination that does not claim divine sanction for itself as the only true embodiment of religion. By this means clergymen and church hierarchies hope to elicit for themselves and their worldly activities an attitude of unquestioning reverence. But such reverence, says Mandeville, is appropriate only to the revealed word of God; for history shows that churches, in interpreting that word, have been as imperfect as any other human institution. To "demonstrate the Difference between Religion and the Church" (169), Mandeville offers a good many historical examples, most of them involving Roman Catholicism. He makes it clear, however, that the Protestant clergy, when given the chance, have been just as ready to twist the gospel to serve their own appetites for secular power. Acknowledging that some Protestants divines "loudly exclaim against the Pomp and Temporal Authority of the Clergy," Mandeville points out that such righteous protests come exclusively from those who are out of power and who would do well "not to boast too much of their Maiden Humility, before they have been tried" (145).

The impulse to tyranny and self-aggrandizement characterizes all priesthoods, whatever their communion; but it does not follow that there is nothing to choose between them. The reasonable man will give his loyal support (though certainly not his blind allegiance) to that church which does least violence to Holy Writ, which best serves the spiritual needs of its adherents, and which eschews the arbitrary exercise of its powers, especially in secular matters. For Mandeville, like the majority of his countrymen, the Church of England most clearly answers these requirements. He insists, however, that the superiority of one church is never in itself sufficient justification for the suppression of another. Schism is unfortunate, but inevitable, for there will always be scrupulous or fanatical persons who disagree with the dominant belief in any country. Splinter religious groups are to be deplored; but, as long as they present no obvious threat to society or to others, they should not be harassed. Admittedly, most heresies are palpably absurd, but this absurdity is all the more reason for pity rather than censure, for "when Men run into Errors, because they are Fools, it is wrong for wise Men to be angry with and punish them, as if they were Knaves" (186).

The repressive measures advocated by some High Churchmen would be infinitely more dangerous than the disease they sought to cure. What is worse, they would almost certainly be ineffective since all experience shows that dissent under persecution is much more likely to become obdurate than weakened. In sum, says Mandeville, "the more a Man knows of the World, either from Reading or Experience, the more he shall be convinc'd, that not only Reveal'd as well as Natural Religion, but likewise Humanity, Reason, the Interest of Mankind, their Peace and Felicity, and almost every thing in Nature pleads for Tolleration, except the National Clergy in every Country" (215).

There is no professional group more deserving of respect and dignity than the clergy when its members are performing their proper tasks of spiritual guidance and moral admonition. But, when clergymen abuse their privileged status by meddling in politics or by enflaming the hatreds of their congregations, it behooves the secular authorities to take strict action. Especially dangerous because their offense is so hard to prosecute are the clergymen whose encitements to violence are delivered by innuendo and gesture:

> To exhort an Audience to Orthodoxy is laudable in a Clergyman; and to bid them beware from Schism, and stand up for the Church, may likewise bear a very good Construction; but if it makes the Mob pull down a Meeting-house in *England,* or abuse Men for having Common Prayer Books in *Scotland,* or commit some other Outrage, would not a Minister of the Gospel, if he was not pleas'd with it, on the first Opportunity undeceive his mistaken Followers, reprove them, that they had misconstrued his Meaning? But if he takes no Notice of it, and goes on in the same Strain against the Sin of Schism; if moreover his pleasant Looks, and a significant Smile now and then cast on the Ringleaders by Stealth, bespeak his Satisfaction, and far from reproving them, with unusual Civilities he seems to reward their Zeal, then what must we think of such a Minister, or what can he say for himself? I should be glad to know what Evasions he can have left, when thus far pursued. (291)

The vividness of this last passage suggests that Mandeville may have witnessed such sermons. The sort of extremist High Churchmen whose pronouncements Defoe had ridiculed in his *Shortest Way With Dissenters* (1702) was still common; indeed, the most notorious High Church incendiary of all —Henry Sacheverell (1674?–1724)—was actively preaching in London at the time Mandeville was writing his *Free Thoughts.* Sacheverell had become famous when in 1709 he had been impeached for a series of sermons in which he denounced the Act of Toleration and issued a thinly disguised call for violence against Dissenters. During the trial his supporters followed his lead by rioting and burning down several Dissenting chapels. Sacheverell was found guilty, but he and his followers interpreted his light sentence (three years suspension from preaching) as a vindication; and, when he resumed his pulpit in 1713 his sermons, though more circumspect in language, continued to convey a tacit invitation to mob violence against schismatics.

I *Political Concerns*

In his final chapters Mandeville addresses himself to several political questions whose religious overtones had made them particularly divisive. By 1720, the doctrine of passive obedience and the divine right of kings had already been rendered partly irrelevant by recent history; but to religious and political conservatives they remained fundamental concerns. Such conservatives argued that the authority of a hereditary monarch was divinely sanctioned and hence was absolute in nature. Accordingly, to rebel against the legitimate ruler, no matter how disagreeable his reign might be, constituted an impermissible act of high sacrilege. To those who held such ideas, the revolutionary settlement of 1688 involved a clear violation of the true line of royal succession, and on this ground a number of Englishmen (mostly of the clergy) refused to swear an oath of allegiance to William and Mary. A generation later there were still those who, within the limits of discretion, publicly questioned the legitimacy of the Hanoverian succession and who privately felt an emotional commitment to the claims of the Pretender.

As we might expect from the liberalism of his earlier stand, Mandeville's position on these matters is Whiggish in character. The doctrine of passive obedience, says Mandeville, arises from a misconception as to where the ultimate power of government should reside. Those who would assign it exclusively to the king are as misguided as those who want to see it vested only in the aristocracy or in the people. Rightly speaking, power should be equally divided between the monarch (representing the broad interests of the nation), the House of Lords (representing the nobility), and the House of Commons (representing the general public): ". . . unlimited Obedience is only due to such Commands, as shall appear to have been given by the joynt Agreement of these three Estates . . ." (300). The king's exercise of power, then, is subject to the cooperation of Parliament; and, if he offends grievously and offers no redress, he himself is violating the law and may be rightly disobeyed.

As to the divine right of kings, Mandeville makes a distinction between the institution of government (which he concedes to be divinely endorsed) and the individual rulers themselves (whose godly credentials he rejects). It is not God's commandment, but rather custom and the desire for social stability, which have dictated the hereditary descent of the crown; and, historically speaking, "All the Quarrels that have been made about the Succession, have ever been decided by the longest Sword" (315). In closing, Mandeville enumerates England's many blessings, and once more warns his readers against being taken in by the religious bigotry and political extremism of fanatical priests.

II *Bayle's Influence*

In the preface to the *Free Thoughts* Mandeville acknowledges his sizeable debt to the skeptical French philosopher, Pierre Bayle (1664–1706):

Those who are vers'd in Books will soon discover, that I have made great Use of Monsieur Baile, without mentioning him.... Had this been done out of Vanity to compliment my self, or disregard to the Honour of that Great Man, I would have been wise enough not to have spoke of it now. The Reasons I had for doing as I have done, are more than one: In the first Place, Monsieur Baile's Dictionary is not common, but among Men who have great Libraries, and quoting it would have signify'd little to the greatest part of my Readers.... Besides, I imagin'd, that it would be unpleasant, if not disgustful, to see the same Name so often repeated in the Notes, especially to those who are unacquainted with the Vastness of that Work. (xv–xvi)[3]

Bayle (likewise acknowledged in the *Fable of the Bees*) had long been a favorite of Mandeville's, not only for the above-mentioned *Dictionnaire historique et critique* (1697) but also for the earlier *Pensées diverses sur la comète* (1682).[4] There is even a possibility that Mandeville, as a schoolboy, may have met Bayle, who in 1685 was teaching at the *École Illustre* in Rotterdam where Mandeville was still in attendance at the Erasmian School.

From Bayle, Mandeville derives a number of premises basic to his ideas on religion and morality, though, like many disciples before and since, Mandeville uses these premises to reach conclusions not necessarily congruent with those of his teacher. In common with Bayle, Mandeville is skeptical as to man's ability either to discover absolute truth or to put into practice such principles of abstract morality as are accessible to him. Both authors maintain that no act, however good its effects, can be called moral if its motives are impure, as on examination they invariably are. Given so rigorous a definition of morality, it follows that *genuine* Christianity is beyond the capabilities of man's corrupt nature; therefore, what passes for religion, particularly as promulgated by churches and priesthoods, deserves no special exemption from critical scrutiny. Within this philosophical framework the unattainable perfection of true religion becomes a strategically valuable standard against which to measure the all-too-apparent imperfections of existing denominations. "Mandeville's work," says Howard Robinson, "is curiously like Bayle's in its lip service to strict morality at the same time that he was proclaiming the impossible and undesirable moral standards he pretended to laud. Mandeville made it hard for his critics to answer him, in the same way that Bayle tantalized his enemies."[5]

III   *The Nature of Mandeville's Belief*

In the heated response which Mandeville's views provoked from his contemporaries it is not unusual to find him categorized as a Deist. Thus, in 1748 Philip Skelton thought it appropriate to entitle his anti-Mandevillean tract *Deism Revealed,* and other authors commonly linked Mandeville's name in denunciation with that of John Toland (1670–1722), the Deist author of *Christianity Not Mysterious* (1696). Yet, even within the broad limits of so imprecise a term, it is difficult to see how Mandeville's religious position can be accurately classified as Deistic. Not only are Mandeville's few direct references to Deism uncomplimentary,[6] but his basic approach to the questions of religion and of human nature is largely antithetical to the benevolent rationalism espoused by the Deists. Early in the *Free Thoughts* Mandeville defines a Deist as one "who believes, in the common Acceptation, that there is a God, and that the World is rul'd by Providence, but has no Faith in any thing reveal'd to us . . ." (3).

As Mandeville's definition suggests, the Deists—insofar as they formed a coherent school at all—were religious rationalists who acknowledged the existence and power of God, but who contended that it was illogical and even impious to believe that He would convey His teachings in such a manner as to put them beyond the comprehension of human reason. Accordingly, the Deists rejected as mere superstition those aspects of Christian doctrine which could not be explained in rational terms. Mandeville, on the other hand, argues the orthodox view that there are certain ultimate truths which unaided reason can never achieve, and for these we must turn to religion. Mysteries which may rightly demand unquestioning acceptance are limited, as Mandeville sees it, to those set forth in the Bible; and he reserves the right to reject any of the postrevelation mysteries insisted on by various priesthoods. But, when God Himself speaks, as He does in the Gospels, then (says Mandeville) we are obliged to accept on faith what we cannot explain by logic.

Thus Mandeville devotes two whole chapters of the *Free Thoughts* to a consideration of such traditional mysteries as the nature of the Trinity and of Free Will verus Predestination. In each case, he finds revelation irreconcilable with logic, from which he does not conclude that the doctrine in question is irrational but rather that is is a suprarational truth of the sort which transcends human understanding. His remarks on the Trinity are characteristic:

What must we do in this Dilemma? Shall we reject part of the Gospel, or say, that there are three Gods, and so speak not only against the clearest Ideas we have of the Deity, but likewise the plainest Doctrine of the same Gospel, as well as of the Old Testament? Not to be guilty of either, we ought to treat this Point with the utmost Diffidence of our Capacity, and fix our Eyes on the eternal Veracity, as well as the unsearchable Wisdom of GOD; and when once we have assured our selves that he cannot have the Will either to deceive us or contradict himself, we shall look upon the whole as a mysterious Truth, which GOD has not been pleased to reveal to us in a more intelligible manner. (66)

The very incomprehensibility of such doctrines becomes for Mandeville an important argument in favor of religious toleration, for, he contends, it is surely presumptuous to try to enforce a conformity of belief on matters essentially unknowable:

The Impossibility there is of reconciling either the System of Predestination, or that of Free-will, to all the necessary Attributes of GOD, ought, if not to unite Men, at least make them desist from Quarreling, and taxing one another with teaching of impious Things and horrid Blasphemies. Those who are against Tolleration of either side, might

be bore with, if they could clearly prove their Opinion, and answer
all Objections after a convincing manner; but that Men should
anathematise, banish and hang those that dissent from them, tho'
their best Solution is GOD's Incomprehensibility, is a Thing altogether inexcusable. (114–115)

The difference between Mandeville's approach to religion
and that of the Deists is apparent also in his concept of human
nature. Concomitant to the Deist's optimistic view of the
capabilities of human reason was a conviction as to the basic
goodness of men. Deistic writers like the Earl of Shaftesbury
(1671–1713) maintained that every man is born with an inherent moral sense which, unless blunted by evil education
or institutions, enables him to recognize what is right and
gives him an instinctive predisposition toward virtue. To
orthodox Christians, committed to a theory which stressed an
innate human sinfulness that could be corrected only by self-
denial and religious instruction, such ideas were abhorrent.
Although Mandeville might differ from religious traditionalists
in many things, he was an insistent as the most rigid High
Churchman about the fundamental selfishness and moral corruption of human nature. He is more often content to describe
than to explain such corruption; but, when he does undertake
to suggest why men are so inclined toward evil, he turns to
the perfectly orthodox idea of original sin.
To call Mandeville a Deist, then, would be palpably inac-
curate, but what those who so described him most often really
meant (and usually went on to say) was that in effect he was
an atheist; and the validity of this latter charge is much more
problematical. Whether or not we consider Mandeville an
atheist will depend largely upon how ready we are to accept
at face value his professions of piety. Most critics—like Robinson in the quotation cited earlier and like myself elsewhere
in this study—have doubted that Mandeville is to be believed
when he claims to advocate the impossibly strict moral standards by which he proves all human activity sinful. By carrying
such doubts only one step further, some readers have concluded (as did so many of Mandeville's contemporaries) that
his repeated avowals of religious belief are actually nothing
more than a mask to disguise what one modern scholar has
called "an insidious persuasion to atheism."[7]

"I would have no Man so uncharitable as to think any Man guilty of Atheism, who does not openly profess it" (3), Mandeville remarks at the beginning of the *Free Thoughts*. The statement is not altogether candid, since Mandeville surely knew that, in an age when the social and legal penalties for atheism were considerable, few men would care to risk a public assertion of disbelief. But it is nevertheless true, as Mandeville later says, that "the Name of Atheist . . . is often abused, and serves . . . for an Instrument of Slander, to defeat an Enemy without further Trouble" (205).

Since at this late date it is hardly possible to speak with certainty on a matter which requires a purely subjective assessment of Mandeville's "sincerity," each reader will no doubt wish to make his own judgment as to the depth and quality of the private faith Mandeville so frequently asserted. It is worth remembering, however, that those who have questioned Mandeville's piety have usually based their opinion not so much upon *what* he says as upon the tone of voice in which he says it. Mandeville's characteristic attitude of amused detachment is so much at odds with the righteous indignation we expect from a man preaching an ascetic morality that readers have always been quick to assume he is simply being satirical toward both the moral code he claims to admire and the religion from which it is derived.

To those in his own day who accused him of privately disbelieving the severe moral standards he publicly espoused, Mandeville replied:

Should it be objected, that I was not in Earnest, when I recommended those mortifying Maxims, I would answer, That those, who think so, would have said the same to St. *Paul*, or JESUS CHRIST himself, if he had bid them sell their Estates and give their Money to the Poor. Poverty and Self-denial have no Allurements in Sight of my Enemies; they hate the Aspect and the very Thoughts of them, as much as they do me; and therefore, whoever recommends them must be in Jest.[8]

Mandeville may not make a very convincing latter-day St. Paul or Jesus; but, as the analogies suggest, there is nothing unprecedented and certainly nothing irreligious about a moral stance which combines ideally maximum demands with realistically minimal expectations. As Thomas R. Edwards, Jr. has observed, "Despite everyone's doubts, I suspect Mandeville may have been a Christian at heart, though in a 'primitive' way that had no use for institutional Christianity—which for him, as for Blake, was only another arm of the secular Establishment."[9]

To say, as Edwards does, that Mandeville "had no use for institutional Christianity" is something of an overstatement. It is true that Mandeville finds fault with all organized religions, and it is also apparent that, despite his nominal Anglicanism, he views the Church of England as barely less objectionable (or perhaps only more convenient) than its generally uninspiring competitors. As indicated earlier, however, he does fully acknowledge the value and importance of churches and clergymen who do not allow minute doctrinal concerns to operate at the expense of basic pastoral functions. The essential requirements for salvation—that we "conquer our Passions, and mortify our Darling Lusts" (8)—remain as obvious and as difficult of achievement as ever; and it is by tirelessly inculcating these immutable moral precepts that any clergyman, whatever his sect, can best serve the interests of society and of true religion:

Few have Leisure and Ability both to read and examine the Scriptures, as they ought, for the thorough understanding of them; and all have not Knowledge sufficient to work out their own Salvation. Vice should be continually expos'd, and Sinners reprov'd, and there is hardly a Christian so mindful of his Duty, as never to stand in need of Admonition, or that he wants not sometimes to be exhorted to true Piety and good Actions. The rude Multitude should be made acquainted with the Heinousness of Sin, and those on whom the Love of GOD has little Influence, and the Joys of Heaven make no Impression, ought to be scar'd from Evil-doing by the Terrors of Hell: For this Reason, no Calling or Profession is so generally useful to a Christian Nation, as the Ministry of the Gospel, and no Set of Men more absolutely necessary than Spiritual Guides, to lead us in the difficult Path of Virtue, and shew us the Way to eternal Happines. (259)

Whatever else we may choose to read into his arguments, Mandeville nowhere suggests that institutional Christianity is unnecessary, but only that it is subject to a full complement of human failings, among which is a notable tendency to exceed its prerogatives.

The force of Mandeville's argument would seem to imply a call for the strict separation of church and state, but in point of fact he makes it clear that he does not question the usefulness and propriety of the Church of England's privileged role as the established state religion—provided, of course, that its clergymen confine their public activities to spiritual matters. Thus, he readily concedes that "A good Government in all Countries pays a deference to the National Church, and no Liberty of Conscience ought to interfere with her just Rights. The publick Temples and Schools ought to be sacred to her, and their Revenues unquestionably due to those only who teach her Doctrine" (244). Mandeville wants to see the established church made as inclusive as possible; but, if conscience still prevents some people from accepting the state religion, they must be prepared to suffer certain disadvantages (though in a just state these will be few):

When Laymen, who cannot Comply with, either the Doctrine or Rites of a Church by Law establish'd, are not stinted in their Birth-right, but enjoy all the Temporal Privileges and Immunities in common with other Subjects, they ought to ask for no more, as to Spiritual Matters, than that they may think what they please, serve GOD in their own way without being disturb'd, be instructed by Teachers of their own Choice, and have the liberty of building Houses for Divine Worship, when and where they think fit. If they make higher demands, which no Layman would think of himself, they ought to be deny'd and rebuk'd, and their Teachers, who put them upon it, corrected. (244)

The religious toleration Mandeville advocates, though considerable, is not without its qualifications. He abhors the persecution of schismatics, and his remark that they should enjoy "Temporal Privileges and Immunities in common with other Subjects" shows that he also has reservations about the numerous civil disabilities which the law imposed (but often failed to enforce) upon those outside the Anglican communion. However, liberty of conscience is one thing; "higher demands" by arrogant minorities are quite another. Mandeville sees no obligation on the state's part to bow before the spiritual pretensions (and much less the secular ambitions) of those outside the established church, especially if, like the Roman Catholics and the Non-Jurors, they refuse "to own the Government to

be the supream Authority upon Earth, both in Church and
State . . . " (241).

Midway in his tract Mandeville remarks that "the Charity
of a Christian in construing the Frailties of others, can hardly
be too extensive" (181). We can well imagine Mandeville's
High Church adversaries wishing that he had been a little
more charitable toward *their* frailties. By the same token, many
among the non-Anglicans whose liberties he defended no
doubt resented his scornful rejection of their more ambitious
claims. Viewed from a modern perspective, however, the
policies Mandeville urges seem both humane and well-
designed to promote his proclaimed goal of minimizing the
social and political disruptions arising from religious animosities. Despite the objections of the pious, history and a growing
segment of influential opinion were on Mandeville's side; and
the ensuing years of the eighteenth century were to see an
increasing acceptance in practice (if not always in theory) of
the secularization of politics he so forcefully advocated in the
*Free Thoughts on Religion, the Church, and National Hap-
piness.*

CHAPTER 6

The Projector

I The "Great Leviathan of Leachery"

AS early as 1714 Mandeville wrote: in "Remark H" of the *Fable of the Bees* that

I am far from encouraging Vice, and think it would be an unspeakable Felicity to a State, if the Sin of Uncleanness could be utterly Banish'd from it; but I am afraid it is impossible: The Passions of some People are too violent to be curb'd by any Law or Precept; and it is Wisdom in all Governments to bear with lesser Inconveniences to prevent greater. If Courtezans and Strumpets were to be prosecuted with as much Rigour as some silly People would have it, what Locks or Bars would be sufficient to preserve the Honour of our Wives and Daughters? . . . some Men would grow outrageous, and Ravishing would become a common Crime. Where six or seven Thousand Sailors arrive at once, as it often happens at *Amsterdam*, that have seen none but their own Sex for many Months together, how is it to be suppos'd that honest Women should walk the Streets unmolested, if there were no Harlots to be had at reasonable Prices? For which Reason the Wise Rulers of that well-ordered City always tolerate an uncertain number of Houses in which Women are hired as publickly as Horses at a Livery-Stable.[1]

Such complacent acceptance of both the inevitability and social utility of prostitution did not sit well with the Grand Jury of Middlesex; and in the formal presentment declaring the *Fable of the Bees* a public nuisance the Grand Jury complained (among other things) that in Mandeville's work "the very *Stews* themselves have had strained Apologies and forced Encomiums made in their Favour and produced in Print, with Design, we conceive, to debauch the Nation."[2] In the *London Journal* for August 10, 1723, Mandeville, who undertook to defend himself, asserted that

The Encomiums upon Stews complained of in the Presentment are no where in the Book. . . . I am sorry the Grand-Jury should conceive that I published this with a Design to debauch the Nation, without considering that in the first Place, there is not a Sentence nor a Syllable that can either offend the chastest Ear, or sully the Imagination of the most vicious; or in the second, that the Matter complained of is manifestly addressed to Magistrates and Politicians, or at least the more serious and thinking Part of Mankind.[3]

One year after this exchange Mandeville—as if to provoke those who had responded so prudishly to his earlier opinions on the subject—amplified and significantly extended those opinions in the *Modest Defence of Publick Stews: Or, an Essay upon Whoring, As It Is Now Practic'd in These Kingdoms.*[4] In the majority of his writings as a social philosopher, Mandeville's approach is that of a diagnostician whose primary concern is with description and analysis rather than with practical reform; and, though the direction of his social and economic sympathies is sufficiently apparent, he rarely embarks on any extended argument in behalf of specific programs of action. In the *Modest Defence,* however, Mandeville not only offers his observations on the delicate social and moral problem of prostitution but also advocates an impressively detailed plan for dealing with it.

In brief, Mandeville's line of argument in the tract is that, despite the efforts of religious reformers, whoring—with its attendant evils of disease, murder of bastard infants, and destruction of moral character—has been greatly on the rise. Restrictive legislation (mostly directed against the shabbier sort of streetwalker) has always been ineffective, since the passion for illicit sex is much too strong ever to be suppressed by mere laws. But, if whoring cannot be eliminated, it can at least be controlled and its social disruptions minimized; and these ends can be best accomplished by the establishment —under parliamentary license and support—of a series of government-operated brothels.

Under such an arrangement, no competition from streetwalkers or independent brothels would be allowed: all prostitutes who either refused or could not qualify to enter a government house would be obliged to give up their profession or face transportation. By such means, "publick whoring" would be kept within orderly confines and its socially noxious side effects sharply curtailed. By the same token, "private whoring" (rape, seduction, and adultery without exchange of money) would be drastically reduced, since few men would be willing to expend time and effort on such activities if they could avail themselves of the cheap, safe, and convenient services of government-approved prostitutes. To so practical and demonstrably desirable a proposal, Mandeville concludes, there can be no serious objection, though it is perhaps possible that some over-scrupulous persons might object that the plan employs immoral means to serve its worthy end. To such, Mandeville answers that, although an individual may rightly be condemned for doing certain evil to produce uncertain good, a legislature cannot be so judged. The actions of the government—whose overriding concern must be for the welfare of society as a whole—can be assessed only by their results; and, if these are beneficial, the act itself must by definition be good. Others may object that by instituting public stews the government will be encouraging vice and hence endangering immortal souls. To this objection Mandeville replies:

> . . . it is universally allow'd as one of the greatest Perfections of the Christian Religion, that its Precepts are calculated to promote the Happiness of Mankind in this World as well as the next; if so, then it is a direct Arraignment of the Lawgivers infinite Wisdom, *i.e.* a Contradiction to assert, that, in Matters of Law and Government, the Publick Breach of any Gospel Precept can possibly be for the temporal Good of any *Society* whatever: And therefore we may with Confidence affirm, that no sinful Laws can be beneficial, and *vice versa*, that no beneficial Laws can be sinful.[5]

In this overt expression of a utilitarian morality the *Modest Defence* is almost unique among Mandeville's works. Although the thrust of Mandeville's social, moral, and political thought nearly always *implies* an unstated utilitarian standard, he typically chooses in the rest of his work to adopt a surface argument wherein morals and religion, rigorously interpreted, are pictured as being inevitably at odds with the demands of worldly society. Yet (as Mandeville's opponents among the pious were quick to see) one way of resolving the paradox that private vices can sometimes lead to public benefits is to revise our ideas of what constitutes vice. By ostensibly embracing the most ascetic ideas of morality, all the while demonstrating how economically disastrous such ideas would be in actual practice, Mandeville in effect offers a tacit argument in favor of a more workable (which is to say, a more latitudinarian) concept of morality. In the *Modest Defence*, however, Mandeville prefers to assume openly the position he elsewhere pretends to deny—namely, that no genuinely beneficial social act can ever be considered contrary to religion or morality.

To account for Mandeville's uncharacteristically direct statement of his position in the *Modest Defence*, F. B. Kaye cites the special requirements of Mandeville's new role as a projector:

In the *Modest Defence* the author is considering a *practical* matter. He is arguing in favor of a definite program, and not simply theorizing. Therefore, had he added to his argument the tag that, however desirable he made his program, it was nevertheless wicked—as Mandeville does in the *Fable*—he would have had no chance of gaining his point. . . . therefore, though he might employ this paradox in a non-propagandistic work such as the *Fable*, where it would be ineffectual to contradict his real desires, [he] would never use it in a book like the *Modest Defence* where it *would* negate them.[6]

Kaye is undoubtedly correct in his assumption that the *Modest Defence*'s plan for government-run prostitution reflects Mandeville's "real desires." As a logical (if not necessarily feasible) answer to a genuine social problem, the proposal bears an authentically Mandevillean stamp. I would suggest, however, that Mandeville was far too realistic ever to suppose that his scheme stood much chance of being adopted and that, accordingly, he is less interested in the *Modest Defence* in convincing his readers of the virtues of his plan than in using the occasion for a series of ironical asides on the related topics of puritanism, sexual economics, and moral reformers.

Had Mandeville entertained any real intentions of winning acceptance for his proposal, he would hardly have presented it in a manner so well-calculated to antagonize the general readers whose support he claims to be soliciting. Government *sponsorship* of brothels (as opposed to mere toleration) is the sort of emotionally charged issue which requires of its advocates a good deal of earnest sobriety and discreet euphemism, assuming that popular persuasion is the desired goal. Mandeville, on the other hand, takes an obvious relish in the humorous possibilities of his subject; and, though his argument remains quite serious in its basic intent, the comic detail with which he surrounds it more clearly suggests the satirist than the propagandist. The very title page gives the reader a fair warning of what to expect, for the ambiguous promise of a "modest" defense of so immodest a subject is at once belied by the punning inscription "Written by a Layman." And this pun is only the first, and perhaps the least scabrous, of the numerous ones which enliven the text—as, for example, when he writes (after a clinically exact discussion of feminine anatomy), "we may conclude ... that Female Chastity is, in its own Nature, built upon a very *ticklish* Foundation" (49).

Mandeville introduces his tract with a mock-dedication to the gentlemen of the Societies for the Reformation of Manners. These were private religious associations whose purpose was the discovery and prosecution of fornicators, blasphemers, sabbath-breakers, and similar moral offenders. So zealous were the members in their activities that in 1735 the London and Westminster societies could boast a forty-year record of no fewer than 99,380 prosecutions for debauchery and profane behavior.[7] As hostile critics of the associations pointed out, however, the purity of motive behind such reform was open to some question, since in many cases informants could legally demand as reward a portion of the offender's fine. Swift—himself a vigorous proponent of moral reform—was reporting a widespread opinion when he remarked in his *Project for the Advancement of Religion* (1708): "Religious Societies, although begun with excellent Intention, and by Persons of true Piety, are said, I know not whether truly or no, to have dwindled into factious Clubs, and grown a Trade to enrich little knavish Informers of the meanest Rank, such as common Constables, and broken Shop-keepers."[8]

Not so much for their hypocrisy as for their ineffectuality does Mandeville twit the societies in his dedication. Unfortunately, the pious harassment of "strolling Damsels" has failed to diminish public lewdness: instead, it has merely served to redirect that lewdness toward more respectable targets. For, as he ruefully comments, "what better could we expect from Your Carting of Bawds, than that the Great Leviathan of Leachery, for Want of these Tubs to play with, should, with one Whisk of his Tail, overset the *Vessel* of

Modesty?" (ii–iii). Characteristic of Mandeville's tone in the dedication are his remarks on the societies's "present Method of Conversion, especially in the Article of Whipping." As one reformer to another, Mandeville helpfully explains: "It is very possible, indeed, that leaving a Poor Girl Penny-less, may put her in a Way of living Honestly, tho' the want of Money was the only Reason of her living otherwise; and the Stripping of her Naked, may, for aught I know, contribute to Her Modesty, and put Her in a State of Innocence; but surely, *Gentlemen*, You must all know, that Flogging has a quite contrary Effect" (x–xi). To the self-righteous puritans of the Societies for Reformation of Manners, it must have seemed altogether appropriate that Mandeville should sign his dedication with the name "Phil-Porny," which is to say, "Lover of Whores."

After a short preface (in which the author assures his audience of the lofty altruism which is his sole motive in writing), the tract itself opens with a seemingly forthright renunciation of any further levity:

There is nothing more idle, or shows a greater Affectation of Wit, than the modern Custom of treating the most grave Subjects with Burlesque and Ridicule. The present Subject of *Whoring*, was I dispos'd, would furnish me sufficiently in this kind, and might possibly, if so handled, excite Mirth in those who are only capable of such low Impressions. But, as the chief Design of this Treatise is to promote the general Welfare and Happiness of Mankind, I hope to be excus'd, if I make no farther Attempts to please, than are consistent with that Design. (1)

As if to reinforce this promise of high seriousness, Mandeville sets about his argument in an orderly, almost legalistic, fashion, compiling methodical lists of current conditions, the virtues of his scheme, answers to possible objections, and so on. The very thoroughness of his approach, however, creates an emphasis which at crucial moments becomes palpably destructive of his announced intention to avoid frivolity. For, though he professes to base his advocacy on the principle that *"of two Evils we ought to chuse the least"* (67), the *real* momentum of his argument is toward proving that government-sponsored brothels will be a *positive good;* and, in support of this theme, he periodically introduces comically extravagant descriptions of the social and sexual benefits his plan will produce.

Among other happy effects, for example, Mandeville pictures the full and satisfying life that government prostitutes will live. Relieved of the economic and physical anxieties of the free-lancer, such courtesans, he predicts, would discover a new sense of pride and fulfillment in their status as respectable civil servants. No longer social outcasts, they would vie with each other to raise professional standards: "It is natural for Mankind to regard chiefly the good Opinion of those with whom they converse, and to neglect that of Strangers; now in this Community [*i.e.*, the state-run brothel], Lewdness not being esteem'd a Reproach, but rather a Commendation, they will set a Value on their good Name, and stand as much upon the Puncto of Honour, as the rest of Mankind; being mov'd by the same commendable Emulation . . ." (18–19).

As for the patrons, not only will they be spared the now prevalent risks of disease and robbery, but they will be able to satisfy their needs inexpensively and without undue neglect of their more important concerns: " . . . if a Man should be overtaken with a sudden Gust of Lechery, it will be no Hindrance to him even in the greatest Hurry of Business, for a ready and willing Mistress will ease him in the twinkling of an Eye, and he may prosecute his Affairs with more Attention than ever, by having his Mind entirely freed and disengag'd from those troublesome Ideas which always accompany a wanton Disposition of the Body" (25–26).

Under the circumstances, it is no wonder that the only possible problem Mandeville can anticipate is that public stews might attract more trade than they can efficiently handle, in which case, he says, Parliament might find it desirable to pass an act *"for encouraging the Importation of foreign Women."* The benefits of such legislation would be manifold: " . . . besides the Honour of our Females, which would be preserv'd by such an Act, it might bring this farther Advantage; That whereas most of our estated Youth spend a great Part of their Time and Fortunes in travelling Abroad, for no other End, as it seems by most of them, but to be inform'd in the *French* and *Italian* Gallantry; they would then have an Opportunity of satisfying their Curiosity in foreign Amours, without stirring out of *London"* (65–66).

Whatever real advantages his scheme might have (and these are quite plausibly argued elsewhere in the tract), Mandeville's

mock-enthusiastic version of happy whores and contented customers is meant as a parody of the kind of glowing predictions
with which his fellow projectors were apt to recommend their
programs. However, it is not merely the naively optimistic
reformer who is parodied in the *Modest Defence;* more specifically, Mandeville here employs for satiric purposes the
manner and apparatus of the mercantilist school of economic
philosophers—a school of which he himself in his other writings is a conspicuous example.

As applied today to early eighteenth-century England, the
term "mercantilist" covers a bewilderingly wide range of
authors on economic theory. But, despite their differences on
points of doctrine, the authors so designated share certain fundamental assumptions, and among these is the belief that the
economic good of the state overshadows the welfare of the
individual. In arguing in support of this principle and the
many proposed policies they derived from it, mercantilist
authors often assumed a dispassionately analytical manner that
was equally offensive to the churchman and to the humani-
tarian. For, in a system of values which measures men and
institutions primarily in terms of their economic utility, there
is very little room left for such commercially unproductive
considerations as religious morality or even human compassion. Instead, the mercantilists cultivated a cool, scientific
detachment in which people in general and the laboring poor
in particular became mere commodities to be dealt with as
unsentimentally as any other economic resource.

Though Mandeville's wit goes a long way toward softening
the harsher implications of the mercantilist ideas which inform
most of his economic writings, he can on occasion be brutally
direct, as in his "Essay on Charity and Charity-Schools" (1723),
where he maintains that:

... in a free Nation where Slaves are not allow'd of, the surest Wealth
consists in a Multitude of laborious Poor.... To make the Society
happy and People easy under the meanest Circumstances, it is requi-
site that great Numbers of them should be Ignorant as well as Poor....
The more a Shepherd, a Plowman or any other Peasant knows of
the World, and the things that are Foreign to his Labour or
Employment, the less fit he'll be to go through the Fatigues and
Hardships of it with Chearfulness and Content.[9]

Among other things, it is the callous indifference to human suffering behind such an attitude that Jonathan Swift so pointedly satirizes in his *Modest Proposal for Preventing the Children of Poor People from being a Burthen to their Parents or Country* (1729).

In making satiric use of a mercantilist approach in the *Modest Defence*, Mandeville is not, of course, trying to discredit that approach, as was Swift in his tract. The purely utilitarian resolution of social problems might bruise the religious and moral sensibilities of some, but what they saw as amorality, Mandeville no doubt thought of as hard-headed realism. Thus, on one level (and that the most important), Mandeville is perfectly serious in his mercantilist contention that the government ought to set itself up in the brothel business. But, serious though he may be, Mandeville is also perfectly aware of the comic potentialities of writing about a subject like prostitution from within a framework of such typically mercantilist preoccupations as quality control, cost estimates, and product distribution. In a happy mercantilist utopia where utility and logic ruled supreme, presumably there would be nothing intrinsically comic or shocking about applying such sensible business criteria to the problems of commercial sex. But until that utopia is achieved, most readers will find such an approach either scandalous or laughable; and Mandeville is at pains to elicit both types of response. Obviously, Mandeville's pretended obliviousness to the incongruity of his treatment involves a degree of self-parody, and in that respect the *Modest Defence* contains an oblique attack upon the humorlessness of some mercantilists. Yet amused as he is at the narrow scientism of his fellow projectors, Mandeville is rather more amused by the predictable nervous laughter and moral outrage (equally squeamish from his point of view) with which he knows much of his audience will react to a briskly rational treatment of a subject society has usually preferred to view emotionally.

Very early in the tract, Mandeville, in effect, announces his philosophical position by citing in support of his proposal a maxim that had been a favorite of mercantilists since the second half of the seventeenth century: namely, that people are the riches of a nation. According to this doctrine (which Mandeville had soberly endorsed a year earlier in the above-quoted "Essay on Charity-Schools"), increase of population is everywhere and at all times desirable, since a large labor force means that wages can be held to a minimum and manufacturing processes kept cheap. As Defoe expressed this view in 1704, " ... the glory, the strength, the riches, the trade, and all that is valuable in a nation as to its figure in the world, depends upon the number of its people, be they never so mean and poor.... "[10]

In the *Modest Defence* Mandeville introduces the subject by pointing out that one of the worst evils of unregulated whoring is that it leads to the murder of bastard children by mothers who are either unwilling to endure the disgrace or loathe to accept the inconvenience of such offspring. With commendable indignation, Mandeville asserts that "a Mind capable of divesting itself so intirely of Humanity, is not fit to live in a civiliz'd Nation." But the reader who applauds this sentiment may find it disconcerting to realize a few lines later that Mandeville is less appalled by the cruelty of infanticide than by its shocking economic wastefulness. This practice, as he points out, "tends very much to dispeople the Country. And since Prosperity of any Country is allow'd to depend, in a great measure, on the Number of its Inhabitants, the *Government* ought, if it were possible, to prevent any Whoring at all, as it evidently hinders the Propagation of the Species" (4–5). The projector in Swift's *Modest Proposal*, it will be recalled, was likewise one who was distressed by the commercial improvidence of murdering unwanted children. But, whereas Swift's irony is meant to expose his projector's moral blindness, Mandeville's intrusive elevation of pragmatic concerns over those of mere morality—here and elsewhere in the tract—is primarily intended to bait the tender-hearted reader.

To this end, he assumes a crisp, businesslike manner, especially in those portions of his pamphlet where he explicates the working details of his proposed brothels. As a man who has obviously given the matter a great deal of thought, he is prepared to give a painstaking rundown of such matters as organizational policy, operating procedure, and personnel management. After modestly conceding that Parliament, "being compos'd of *Spirituals* as well as *Temporals*" (12), will no doubt wish to add its own embellishments, he spells out the mechanics of his proposal. London, he estimates, will require at least one hundred houses, each containing twenty prostitutes and a resident matron "of Abilities and Experience." Conveniently nearby will be an infirmary staffed by two physicians and four surgeons, and supervising all will be three royal commissioners whose job will be "to hear and redress Complaints, and to see that each House punctually observes such Rules and Orders as shall be thought Necessary for the good Government of this Community" (13). By way of encouraging trade, "each House must be allow'd a certain Quantity of all sorts of Liquor, Custom and Excise free; by which Means they will be enabled to accommodate Gentlemen handsomely, without that Imposition so frequently met with in such Houses" (13).

Building enthusiasm as he gets down to crucial money matters, Mandeville explains that:

For the better Entertainment of all Ranks and Degrees of Gentlemen, we shall divide the twenty Women of each House into four Classes, who for their Beauty, or other Qualifications may justly challenge different Prices.

The first Class is to consist of eight, who may legally demand from each Visitant Half a Crown. The second Class to consist of six, whose fix'd Price may be a Crown. The third Class of four, at half a Guinea each. The remaining two make up the fourth Class, and are design'd for Persons of the first Rank, who can afford to Pay a Guinea for the Elegancy of their Taste. (13–14)[11]

Further employing the sort of statistical computations and "political arithmetic" so favored by mercantilist writers, Mandeville points out that "To defray the Charges of this Establishment, will require but a very moderate Tax: For if the first Class pays but forty Shillings Yearly, and the rest in Proportion, it will amount to above ten thousand Pounds a Year, which will not only pay the Commissioners Salaries, Surgeons Chests, and other Contingencies, but likewise establish a good Fund for the Maintenance of Bastard-Orphans and superannuated Courtezans" (14).

Discipline will be strictly enforced, with each matron empowered to see to it that no girl leaves without permission and that disorderly or drunken patrons are refused admission. Recruitment of working staff, Mandeville says, will present no problems, other than perhaps at first an embarrassment of riches, for "the vast Choice and Variety . . . of these Women, will give us an Opportunity of making a very beautiful Collection" (63–64). But, if ever the day should come when "Supplies should not prove sufficient to answer the greatness of the Demand," the worst that can happen is that frustrated customers will go back to seducing virgins, which practice, Mandeville triumphantly points out, will in time produce a whole new crop of potential employees for the public stews.

As befits a physician, Mandeville is particularly concerned that hygenic standards be maintained: "For the *Society*'s Security in Point of Health, it must be order'd, That if any Gentleman complains of receiving an Injury, and the Woman, upon Search, be found tainted, without having discover'd it to the Mistress, she shall be stripp'd and cashier'd. But if a Woman discovers her Misfortune before any Complaint is made against her, she shall be sent to the *Infirmary*, and cured at the Publick Charge. No Woman that has been twice pox'd shall ever be re-admitted" (14–15). With a nice sense of distinction, Mandeville adds to these medical regulations the explanatory comment, *"Note,* That three Claps shall be reckon'd equivalent to one Pox" (14).

In the preface to his tract Mandeville had told his readers: *"I am in some pain for the Event of this* Scheme, *hoping the* Wicked *will find it too Grave, and fearing the* Godly *will scarce venture beyond the Title-Page: And should they even, I know they'll object, 'tis here and there interwoven with too ludicrous Expressions, not considering that a dry Argument has occasion for the larding of Gaiety to make it the better relish and go down"* (xiv).

Not all the *Modest Defence of Publick Stews* is written with a *"larding of Gaiety,"* but, as I have tried to show, even in his most sober passages Mandeville has a way of moving from earnest advocacy to a sly parody of it. Knowing, as he did, that the "Godly" adherents of the Societies for the Reformation of Manners were likely to find his proposal offensive even without its satiric trimmings, Mandeville shrewdly concluded that he had nothing to lose by couching his basically serious argument in terms that would enable him to share his amusement at what he saw as the irrationality and hypocrisy of society's attitude toward sex in general and prostitution in particular.

II   *The "Fatal Tree"*

In the *British Journal* for February 27, 1725, there appeared, under the name "Philanthropos," the first of six weekly letters dealing with England's growing crime rate and proposing reforms in the treatment and disposition of convicted felons. Public attention toward matters of crime and its punishment had been heightened only a few months earlier by the much-publicized hanging of the famous burglar, Jack Sheppard, and the letters of "Philanthropos" achieved an added timeliness when, as if in counterpoint to their publication, there took place the arrest (February 15, 1725) and the execution (May 24, 1725) of the notorious "thief-taker general," Jonathan Wild.

Shortly after their initial appearance in the *British Journal* the six letters (this time signed "*B. Mandeville*, M.D.") were issued together in a pamphlet bearing the full title *An Enquiry into the Causes of the Frequent Executions at Tyburn: and a Proposal for some Regulations concerning Felons in Prison, and the good Effects to be Expected from them. To Which is Added, a Discourse on Transportation, and a Method to render that Punishment more Effectual.* As he had the year before in the *Modest Defence,* Mandeville assumes the role of projector, but in the *Enquiry* neither the proposals nor the manner in which Mandeville presents them are deliberately calculated to offend or amuse. Unlike its predecessor, the *Enquiry* is a practical effort at achievable reform, and Mandeville accordingly takes care to avoid unseemly comedy as he explains how society may "lessen if not prevent the common Practice of Thieving, and save many Lives of the loose and indigent Vulgar, of which now such great Numbers are yearly lavish'd away for Trifles."[12]

Mandeville ascribes the upsurge in crime to "two palpable Evils, distinct from those we have in common with other large overgrown Cities. One regards Prosecutions; the other the Treatment that is given to Malefactors after they are taken" (2). To the first of these he addresses himself in his opening chapter: "*Of* Theftbote; *or the Crime of Compounding of Felony.*" The term "theftbote" (or "theftboot") designated the taking of payment—usually the return of stolen goods—from a thief in exchange for money and an agreement not to prosecute. In common practice, the victim of a robbery might insert

a notice in the newspaper specifying his loss and offering
a "reward" with no questions asked to anyone who could assist
him. In describing such advertisements Mandeville allows
himself one of the few passages of sustained irony in the tract:

The Tenor of them is rather benevolent than injurious: And a Panegy-
rist on the present Times might justly say of them, That in no Perfor-
mances the true Spirit of Christianity was so conspicuous as in these:
That they were not only free from Calumny and ill Language, but
likewise so void of Reproach, that speaking to a Thief, we never
call'd him so in those charitable Addresses: That in them the very
Catalogues of Injuries receiv'd, were penn'd with as little Heat, or
Resentment, as ever Tradesman shew'd in a Bill of Parcels directed
to his best Customer: That here we are so far from hating our Enemy,
that we proffer him a Recompence for his Trouble, if he will conde-
scend to let us have our own again; and leaving all Revenge to God,
to shew that we are willing to forgive and forget, we consult, in
the most effectual Manner, the Safety of a Person that deserves Hanging for the Wrong he has done us. (4–5)

Such exchanges between a thief and his victim, says Mandeville, are pernicious because they encourage crime by making it safe and profitable. But even more detrimental to society
is the refinement of simple theftbote into a well-organized
business, as exemplified by the remarkable career of Jonathan
Wild. Wild (1682?–1725) had begun as a receiver of stolen
goods and as a thief-taker—that is, an informant who was paid
a reward for the criminals he turned in. When laws were passed
increasing the penalties for receiving stolen goods, Wild
developed a system whereby thieves, instead of bringing him
their booty, would merely inform him of what they had taken.
Acting as a broker (and thus not violating any law), Wild would
approach the victim and arrange for a price to have his belong-
ings returned.

So flourishing was his trade that in time Wild became a
veritable potentate of crime. He recruited individual robbers
into specialized gangs; established warehouses in which to
store what was stolen; and, from his office in Cock Alley (where
robbery victims now came to *him*), he sold the merchandise
back to its original owners. In addition, Wild continued his
activities as a thief-taker, thus furnishing himself with a profitable sideline and a valuable disciplinary measure against crim-

inals who proved insufficiently cooperative. Though special laws were passed to trap him, he evaded these by slightly revising his methods of operation; and his eventual downfall (which so opportunely coincided with the publication of Mandeville's *Enquiry)* was based on a legal technicality.[13] Such wholesale entrepreneurs of crime as Wild, Mandeville maintains, would soon cease to function if strict laws were passed to make it criminal for "any Man, for Lucre, to connive at a Piece of Felony which he could have hinder'd" (9).

Mandeville's indictment of theftbote occupies less than one third of the fifty-five page *Enquiry,* the rest of which is devoted to the second of the "two palpable Evils" contributing to crime—the treatment accorded felons after their capture. Prisoners in Newgate, Mandeville points out, are not segregated by age, sex, or offence, but are instead promiscuously assembled in unruly groups as large as forty or fifty. Discipline is very lax, and only the destitute or inexperienced are obliged to live on the meager prison fare: "Veteran Rogues" always see to it that ample food and drink is sent them by friends on the outside. The crowding, drunkenness, and debauchery create an environment in which the genuine contrition and religious soul-searching which *should* take place in prison become all but impossible. After the moral squalor of such imprisonment, it is sadly appropriate that those criminals who are condemned to death should make their exits in a manner which is a travesty of the dignity that ought to characterize so solemn an occasion.

Since the public execution of criminals is a subject central to Mandeville's thesis, he devotes most of chapters two and three to a vivid description and analysis of the ceremony itself and its putative effects. In theory, the public hanging of malefactors at the Tyburn gallows was intended not merely to punish the guilty but, more importantly, to deter potential wrong-doers by forcibly demonstrating the terrible consequences of crime. In practice, however, such executions had by Mandeville's time become what they were to remain throughout most of the eighteenth century—frenzied and disorderly spectacles which the mob enjoyed as a kind of sporting event.

The hanging of Jack Sheppard on November 16, 1724—still fresh in the minds of Mandeville's readers—epitomized the carnival atmosphere which "Tyburn Fair" had come to assume. Sheppard's courage as a thief and the boldness he had shown in a series of earlier escapes from prison had made him so popular a hero that during his final imprisonment his guards earned no less than two hundred pounds by exhibiting him to the curious at four shillings a head. On the day of his execution, he was wildly cheered by the crowd as, already wearing the noose fixed around his neck, he climbed aboard the cart which he shared with a clergyman, the hangman, and a coffin on the way to Tyburn. Preceded by a posse of constables and followed by a troop of soldiers and more constables, the procession noisily made its way to the church of St. Sepulchre, where, after a short prayer, Sheppard was tossed the customary flowers and ribbons from the church steps. After a second stop—this time, as tradition demanded, at a tavern for drinks —the procession arrived at Tyburn, having taken almost three hours to negotiate the two and one-half mile distance. On the scaffold, facing the permanent grandstands which had been erected for such events, Sheppard was subjected to religious exhortations and encouraged to sing psalms and to confess his sins. Contributing to the entertainment of the crowd were the usual hawkers of gin, food, and the numerous biographies, confessions, and ballads hastily issued by Grub Street. After the hanging, Sheppard's body was cut down by friends who hoped to resuscitate him, but they were prevented by the mob which mistakenly thought that the body was being taken to an anatomist for dissection.[14]

One eye-witness estimated that some two-hundred thousand people had attended the "turning off" of Jack Sheppard, and it is not unlikely that Bernard Mandeville was one of them. In any case, he had clearly been present on many similar occasions, and in his description of a typical hanging day he powerfully recreates the entire brutal spectacle. Far from being penitent, most condemned men, says Mandeville, are nearly insensible from drink, which accounts for their air of composure so admired by the mob. The crowd itself is also largely intoxicated, not merely on the cheap gin, but on the sadistic excitement whose sexual overtones do not escape Mandeville's observant eye: "All the Way, from *Newgate* to *Tyburn*, is one continued Fair, for Whores and Rogues of the meaner Sort. Here the most abandon'd Rakehells may light on Women as shameless: Here Trollops, all in Rags, may pick up Sweethearts of the same Politeness: And there are none so lewd, so vile, or so indigent, of either Sex, but at the Time and Place aforesaid, they may find a Paramour" (20).

The hideous noise and confusion at the gallows present wonderful opportunities for the hordes of pickpockets and cutpurses who industriously ply the trades that will one day earn them their own turn on the scaffold. In such circumstances, it is not surprising that the actual hangings produce neither terror nor pious reflection among the spectators, most of whom find the event more gruesomely festive than morally instructive. As a physician, Mandeville finds it strange that the mob —so often without any compassion for the condemned criminals—becomes furiously protective of their corpses when anatomists try to purchase their bodies for dissection. "They have suffer'd the Law, (cries the Rabble,) and shall have no other Barbarities put upon them: We know what you are, and will not leave them before we see them buried" (26). In urging that the "superstitious Reverence of the Vulgar for a Corpse" be disregarded and that the bodies of all criminals be made available to surgeons, Mandeville assures his readers that "The Dishonour would seldom reach beyond the Scum of the People; and to be dissected, can never be a greater Scandal than being hanged" (27).

Mandeville contends that public executions of the sort described not only fail to discourage crime but, in fact, contribute greatly to its increase. The crowd makes heroes of those who show little fear on the gallows, and thus it becomes a point of pride with the condemned to face death without flinching. But such stoicism, while admirable in an innocent martyr, is grossly inappropriate on the part of a guilty sinner about to suffer a just retribution. As things stand, however, the rare criminal who gives evidence of a sensible terror over his approaching damnation becomes the target of contemptuous abuse from a mob which ignorantly applauds brazen impenitence, surly defiance, and drunken stupor as if they were courage. The seeming imperturbability of so many of the condemned, says Mandeville, leads many impressionable spectators to conclude that hanging must be an easy price to pay for the fame, excitement, and profit of a criminal career.

Though society cannot hope to eradicate crime, measures

can be taken to inhibit its growth; and with that purpose in mind Mandeville, "without Arrogance or Presumption," proposes a series of regulations concerning the treatment of convicted felons. He urges that each prisoner be confined in a separate cell, searched every night, and denied all access to his fellow inmates. Since hardened sinners seldom repent as long as they entertain the slightest hope of deliverance, a law should be passed fixing a certain period beyond which the condemned would no longer be subject to either pardon or reprieve. After that period has expired, the prisoner should be allowed one day to say goodby to his family, and then three days in which to make his peace with God. From the day that the date of his execution is announced, the prisoner should be placed on a strict diet of bread and water, so that, "free from Fumes of Food, and all intoxicating Comforts" (41), he may contemplate his guilt.

Among the desirable effects of such regulations, Mandeville predicts that public executions would begin to assume their proper function as grim object lessons:

When a Man thus wean'd from the World, and all the Hopes of Life, should be drawn forth from his dark and solitary Dungeon, once more enjoy the open Air, and see himself exposed to gazing Multitudes, there met on purpose to feed their Curiosity at his Expence; when the Paleness of his Countenance, and the Shaking of every Limb, should, without Disguise, reveal the Motions of his Heart; and his Spirits neither confounded, nor buoy'd up by inebriating Liquors, should discover their real Condition and Incapacity to uphold their trembling Tenement; the Spectacle would be awful, and strike the Hearts of the Beholders: When seated on the ignominious Cart, by his restless Posture, the Distortion of his Features, and the continual wringing of his Hands, he should disclose his Woe within, and the utmost depth of Sorrow: When we should hear his shrill Cries and sad Complaints interrupted with bitter Sobs and anxious Groans, and now and then, at sudden Starts, see Floods of Tears gushing from his distracted Eyes, how thoroughly would the Concurrence of so many strong Evidences convince us of the Pangs, the amazing Horror, and unspeakable Agonies of his excruciated Soul! (41–42)

With the terrible wages of sin so clearly demonstrated, crime would attract fewer recruits; and, as a result, executions themselves would in time be brought to an irreducible minimum.

Mandeville's concluding chapter deals with "transportation"—that system whereby lesser malefactors were sent overseas (primarily to America or the West Indies) to spend their sentences in forced agricultural labor. Mandeville feels that transportation, though admirable in concept, has been ineffective in practice. Escapes are numerous, and plantation owners complain that criminals "do very little Service themselves, and spoil the other Slaves, teaching the *Africans* more Villany and Mischief than ever they could have learn'd without the Examples and Instructions of such *Europeans*" (47).

Mandeville proposes that prisoners, instead of being transported to British colonies, should be shipped to North Africa and exchanged for the English seamen who have been captured by Barbary Coast pirates and made slaves. Such a transaction, says Mandeville, would serve both justice and expediency, for by it the innocent would be liberated and the guilty at last made useful. The North Africans would in all likelihood be amenable, since they value physical strength more than moral character in their slaves. Admittedly, the punishment would be a terrible one, though "There would ... be room always, with fresh Supplies of Felons, to release those, who might be cured, or, at least, thought to have been sufficiently punish'd" (51). In any case, only by making the consequences of crime dreadful can society protect itself; and Mandeville is confident that this reform, in conjunction with all the others he has suggested, will work effectively toward that desirable end.

Today, some two and one-half centuries after its composition, it is difficult to read Mandeville's *Enquiry* without a sense of horror—both at the brutality of eighteenth-century penal practices (which Mandeville finds so lenient) and at the additional rigors he advocates as corrective measures. Our dismay is heightened by the knowledge that in Mandeville's time a large percentage of those condemned to death were guilty of acts which would today be considered little more than misdemeanors. Previous to 1688 the number of capital offences in England had been about fifty, but during the course of the eighteenth century the number more than quadrupled, as new items were added in haphazard response to the growing incidence of crime against property. It was punishable by hanging to steal a sheep or a horse; to rob to the value of forty shillings or more from a dwelling; to take five shillings in value from a shop; or to steal as little as twelve pence in value from a pocket.

Aside from the severity of such laws, the criminal code was almost whimsical in its detail. A person could be executed for stealing forty shillings from a vessel on a navigable river, but not if he waited until the vessel had moved on to a canal. It was a capital offense to steal fruit that had been gathered, but it was only a trespass to gather it oneself and steal it.[15] Though the harshness and inconsistency of the law sometimes made juries reluctant to convict, the hapless pickpockets and shoplifters by far outnumbered the murderers among the men, women, and even children who made the nightmarish journey to "Tyburn Tree." Stealing a lace handkerchief from someone's pocket may well be a terrible thing, but to most modern readers—less appalled by such a theft than by the savagery of the criminal code that made it a capital offense—Mandeville's *Enquiry* is apt to seem callous in its assumptions and barbaric in its proposals.

Without necessarily denying the justice of such charges, it is only fair to reiterate that Mandeville's opinions on criminology are the conventional ones of his time. In almost every case, contemporary pamphlets and Parliamentary reports on the subject assumed as a matter of course that the best way to control crime was to make punishment terrible. When crime continued to grow, the usual response was not to reexamine the premise but to urge increasingly severe legal penalties. With the sole exception of his proposal that felons be traded into slavery, none of Mandeville's suggested penal reforms was original with him, nor, in the light of prevailing opinion, were they especially extreme. When Henry Fielding addressed himself to the problem in his *Enquiry into the Causes of the late Increase of Robbers* (1751), most of his conclusions and even his specific proposals were largely identical with those Mandeville had put forward twenty-six years before.

Harsh as Fielding's and Mandeville's attitudes may appear today, they seem positively benign when compared to those of such writers as the anonymous author of *Hanging not Punishment enough, for Murtherers, High-way Men, and House-*

Breakers (1701), a tract which suggests that society would benefit if certain criminals were broken on the wheel, whipped to death, or hanged alive in chains to die of starvation and exposure. No less zealous was George Ollyffe, whose *Essay Humbly Offer'd for an Act of Parliament to prevent Capital Crimes* (1731) advocates the elaborate public torture of prisoners. Not many, perhaps, were quite so ferocious; but in 1783, when the procession to Tyburn was abolished, even the humane Samuel Johnson disapproved. Reformers, he told Sir William Scott, "object that the old method drew together a number of spectators. Sir, executions are intended to draw spectators. If they do not draw spectators they don't answer their purpose. The old method was most satisfactory to all parties; the publick was gratified by a procession; the criminal was supported by it. Why is all this to be swept away?" To which Boswell, himself a frequent spectator at executions, comments: "I perfectly agree with Dr. Johnson upon this head, and am persuaded that executions now, the solemn procession being discontinued, have not nearly the effect which they formerly had."[16]

If Mandeville, then, is to be criticized as unfeeling, it can at least be said in his defense that the callousness he displays is shared in one degree or another by most of his contemporaries. For that matter, Mandeville's fundamental attitudes toward crime and its punishment are not uncommon ones today, though modern proponents of such views customarily avoid the blunt directness of Mandeville's approach. To cite mitigating factors, however, is not to deny that in some parts of the *Enquiry* Mandeville does show a disagreeably obvious relish in anticipating the suffering that criminals will undergo once his recommendations have been put into effect. Thus, at one point, Mandeville enthusiastically predicts that his proposed regimen of solitary confinement on a diet of bread and water might prove so conducive to spirituality that condemned men would be inspired to deliver heart-felt sermons from the scaffold. As he envisages such edifying occasions,

Sometimes they would deter the wicked and in the same Breath solicite Heaven for their Conversion: At others, reasoning from the Changes they had experienced within, they would combat Impiety with Vehemence, and conjure Unbelievers no longer to doubt of an everlasting Futurity: They would paint to them, in the strongest

Colours, the Horrors they had felt from an accusing Conscience, and
the Abyss of Misery they had been plunged in, whilst yet labouring
under the dire Reflection on eternal Vengeance; And thus, mixing
fervent Prayers with strenuous Exhortation, they would employ the
few Moments, that were left them, in Exercises intirely spiritual and
holy.

How such Conversations would affect the Minds of all that saw
or heard them, cannot be better imagin'd than by examining our
selves. When we had seen an half-starv'd Wretch, that look'd like
Death, come shivering from his Prison, and hardly able to speak
or stand, get with Difficulty on the slow uncomfortable Carriage;
where, at the first Rumbling of it, he should begin to weep, and
as he went, dissolve in Tears, and lose himself in incoherent Lamenta-
tions, it would move us to Compassion. But with what Astonishment
would it not fill us, to behold the same Creature, near the fatal Tree,
become lively, glow with Zeal, and, in Strength of Voice and Action,
excell the most vigourous Preachers! (45–46)

It is a notable irony—though perhaps a not altogether uninten-
tional one—that such a passage should be so reminiscent of
the kind of pious sadism for which Mandeville had previously
ridiculed the Societies for the Reformation of Manners.

What most recommends the *Enquiry* to readers today, however, is not its archaic criminology nor still less its chilling
proposals: rather it is Mandeville's vivid description of the
grimly fascinating events of a typical execution day. With his
talent for striking detail, Mandeville has created a series of
sharply observed scenes which the reader experiences with
the immediacy of an actual participant in the shouting, pushing
mob. The confusion at Newgate, for example, is conveyed
by the following rapid succession of images:

The horrid Aspects of Turnkeys and Gaolers, in Discontent and Hurry;
the sharp and dreadful Looks of Rogues, that beg in Irons, but would
rob you with greater Satisfaction, if they could; the Bellowings of
half a dozen Names at a time, that are perpetually made in the
Enquiries after one another; the Variety of strong Voices, that are
heard, of howling in one Place, scolding and quarrelling in another,
and loud Laughter in a third; the substantial Breakfasts that are made
in the midst of all this; the Seas of Beer that are swill'd; the never-
ceasing Outcries for more; and the bawling Answers of the Tapsters
as continual; the Quantity and Varieties of more extoxicating Liquors,
that are swallow'd in every Part of *Newgate;* the Impudence, and
unseasonable Jests of those, who administer them; their black Hands,

and Nastiness all over; all these, joined together, are astonishing and terrible, without mentioning the Oaths and Imprecations, that from every Corner are echo'd about, for Trifles; or the little, light, and general Squallor of the Gaol itself, accompany'd with the melancholy Noise of Fetters, differently sounding, according to their Weight. (18–19)

The raucous procession to the gallows elicits these Hogarthian vignettes:

Now you see a Man, without Provocation, push his Companion in the Kennel; and two Minutes after, the Sufferer trip up the other's Heels, and the first Aggressor lies rolling in the more solid Mire: And he is the prettiest Fellow among them, who is the least shock'd at Nastiness, and the most boisterous in his Sports. No modern Rabble can long subsist without their darling Cordial, the grand Preservative of Sloth, *Jeneva,* that infallible Antidote against Care and frugal Reflexion; which, being repeated removes all Pain of sober Thought, and in a little Time cures the tormenting Sense of the most pressing Necessities. The Traders, who vent it among the Mob on these Occasions, are commonly the worst of both Sexes, but most of them weather-beaten Fellows, that have mis-spent their Youth. Here stands an old Sloven, in a Wig actually putrify'd, squeez'd up in a Corner, and recommends a Dram of it to Goers-by: There another in Rags, with several Bottles in a Basket, stirs about with it, where the Throng is the thinnest, and tears his Throat with crying his Commodity; and further off, you may see the Head of a third, who has ventur'd in the Middle of the Current, and minds his Business, as he is fluctuating in the Irregular Stream: Whilst higher up, an old decrepit Woman sits dreaming with it on a Bulk; and over against her, in a Soldier's Coat, her termagant Daughter sells the Sots-Comfort with great Dispatch. (20–21)

To the historian, Mandeville's tract is primarily valuable as a representative social document; but, to the student of literature, it is the powerful realism of descriptive passages like those above which gives the *Enquiry into the Causes of the Frequent Executions at Tyburn* its strongest claim to continued attention.

CHAPTER 7

Fable of the Bees

IN the 1714 preface to the *Fable of the Bees* Mandeville remarks: "If you ask me, why I have done all this, . . . and what Good these Notions will produce? truly, besides the Reader's Diversion, I believe, none at all. . . . "[1] Over the years the *Fable of the Bees* grew steadily in scope as well as in size, but Mandeville continued to profess that the book he referred to as "this little Whim" (I, 9) and "this Amusement" (I, 369) had been designed less for the instruction of its readers than for their casual entertainment. Needless to say, didacticism plays a much more central role in the *Fable of the Bees* than Mandeville's remarks would imply; but it is nonetheless true that Mandeville, though basically quite serious, is anything but solemn in his approach.

Even those readers who are repelled by his ideas have on occasion been willing to testify to the humor and high spirits of what Henry Crabb Robinson thought was "the wickedest cleverest book in the English language."[2] To Robinson's opinion, we may add that of Leslie Stephen, whose acknowledgment of Mandeville's wit is all the more convincing for the obvious reluctance with which it is made. That Stephen felt he *ought* not to be amused by the *Fable of the Bees* is clear from his comment:

Mandeville is said to have been in the habit of frequenting coffeehouses and amusing his patrons by ribald conversation. The book smells of its author's haunts. He is a cynical and prurient writer, who shrinks from no jest, however scurrilous, and from no paradox, however grotesque, calculated to serve the object—which he avows in his preface to be his sole object—of amusing his readers; readers, it may be added, far from scrupulous in their tastes.[3]

But, having so firmly expressed his distaste for Mandeville's coarseness, Stephen ends his essay with the rather grudging admission that Mandeville, "if the truth must be spoken, has, after all, written a very amusing book."[4]

In Mandeville's own day, however, it was not amusement but outrage which was the dominant public response to the *Fable of the Bees*. That Mandeville's work should have been adversely received by an age increasingly prone to resent attacks upon the "dignity of human nature"[5] is hardly a matter for surprise; but, if the hostility of Mandeville's contemporaries was predictable, its vast dimensions and vehemence were not. No English author since Thomas Hobbes had touched so raw a nerve, and men who agreed in almost nothing else became united in their condemnation of Mandeville. Even Swift, who in *Gulliver's Travels* set out deliberately to vex the world, met with less widespread indignation than Mandeville, who ostensibly sought only to divert it.

Part of the special quality that for most readers made Mandeville so much more offensive than Swift is suggested by Stephen in the essay just quoted. "Mandeville," Stephen writes, "shares Swift's contempt for the human race, but his contempt, instead of urging him to the confines of madness, finds easy vent in a horse-laugh. He despises himself as well as his neighbours, and is content to be despicable. He is a scoffer, not a misanthrope. You are all Yahoos, he seems to say, and I am a Yahoo; and so—let us eat, drink, and be merry."[6] Stephen's paraphrase is less than fair to Mandeville, who nowhere issues the invitation to license ascribed to him. But it is certainly true that Mandeville—in conspicuous contrast to Swift—responds to the spectacle of human sin and folly with a degree of good-humored equanimity that makes his formal expressions of disapproval seem perfunctory. Even Mandeville's insistence on the symbiotic relationship between vice and national greatness would have shocked fewer readers had he coupled it (as did Swift in making much the same general point) with a more convincing display of disapprobation. What is missing from Mandeville—or at least so muted as to be imperceptible to most who read him[7]—is the basic *saeva indignatio* that gives Swift's vision of human corruption its characteristic moral intensity.

I The Satiric Gadfly

In Mandeville's replies to critics, he often affected an air of wounded innocence, professiong himself amazed that so inoffensive a work as the *Fable* should ever have inspired so much hostility. Mandeville's whole career, however, suggests how much he relished the role of satiric gadfly; even a casual reading of his book reveals the care he has taken to present his case, especially in its details, in a way calculated to discomfit his audience. Even those of his contemporaries who were inclined to accept the general substance of Mandeville's argument must have sometimes bridled at what Kaye describes as the "humorously cynical downrightness of statement that made him so provocative that even now, after two hundred years, he has kept almost unimpaired his ability to irritate those who disagree with him" (I, cxxxv–cxxxvi).

A characteristic example of Mandeville's approach is his assertion that

The Fire of *London* was a great Calamity, but if the Carpenters, Bricklayers, Smiths, and all, not only that are employed in Building but likewise those that made and dealt in the same Manufactures and other Merchandizes that were Burnt, and other Trades again that got by them when they were in full Employ, were to Vote against those who lost by the Fire; the Rejoicings would equal if not exceed the Complaints. In recruiting what is lost and destroy'd by Fire, Storms, Sea-fights, Sieges, Battles, a considerable part of Trade consists. (I, 359)

Mandeville's point in this passage, if stated proverbially ("It's an ill wind that blows no good"), becomes simply banal; or, if put in the form of a general proposition ("The task of reconstruction after a public disaster contributes to economic recovery"), it remains unexceptional. In neither case would the idea be likely to inspire much objection. But Mandeville—by citing an explicit example so painfully close to home and by carefully emphasizing the benefits of disaster without giving more than passing attention to its horrors—has seen to it that the idea assumes an uncompromising bluntness that greatly increases its potential for provocation.

We can see the same kind of process at work in the group of prose "Remarks" which Mandeville wrote in order to explicate the original *Grumbling Hive*. These essays illustrate Mandeville's contention that the morality of the Ten Commandments is not compatible with the requirements of a money-making society. "I write not to many, nor seek for any Well-wishers, but among the few that can think abstractly . . . " (I, 231), says Mandeville in "Remark T." From such an assertion we might expect that Mandeville's emphasis would be on the enunciation of general philosophical principles. Certainly, these are not lacking in the work; but, if we examine the "Remarks" themselves, we find that the greater part of each concerns a series of very particular and concrete illustrations. Moreover, these illustrations are selected and expressed in a way more strongly suggestive of the *agent provocateur* than of the abstract philosopher.

"Remark C," for example, is written by way of a gloss on the relatively innocuous lines from *Grumbling Hive:* "The Soldiers, that were forc'd to fight,/If they surviv'd, got Honour by't" (I, 22). That men should be willing to receive praise for what they would gladly have avoided had they been able leads Mandeville to conclude that what men call honor is a reflection not of moral reality but of public opinion. By the same token, says Mandeville, the dominant factor when we feel shame is not the awareness of our own unworthiness but simply the discomfort we experience when we fear that others may recognize that unworthiness.

To illustrate these points and their corollaries, Mandeville does not limit himself to abstractions nor does he draw his examples (as his opening seems to promise) from the battlefield. Instead, he turns to the much more lively and (for most readers) much more sensitive topic of sexual behavior. Thus, we are informed that virgins who blush at bawdiness do so not out of innocence, but simply out of fear that they may inadvertently reveal the impurity of their inner thoughts and desires. To demonstrate how men and women acquire rather than inherit their ideas of modesty, Mandeville explains: "*Miss* is scarce three Years old, but she is spoke to every Day to hide her Leg, and rebuk'd in good Earnest if she shews it; while *Little Master* at the same Age is bid to take up his Coats, and piss like a Man" (I, 72).

No less piquant is Mandeville's ensuing example of the way social convention, rather than intrinsic moral content, dictates society's judgment of its members's actions:

If a Man should tell a Woman, that he could like no body so well to propagate his Species upon, as her self, and that he found a violent Desire that Moment to go about it, and accordingly offer'd to lay hold of her for that purpose; the Consequence would be, that he would be call'd a Brute, the Woman would run away, and himself never be admitted in any civil Company. . . . But a Man need not conquer his Passions, it is sufficient that he conceals them. . . . A fashionable Gentleman may have as violent an Inclination to a Woman as the brutish Fellow; but then he behaves himself quite otherwise; he first addresses the Lady's Father, and demonstrates his Ability splendidly to maintain his Daughter; upon this he is admitted into her Company, where, by Flattery, Submission, Presents, and Assiduity, he endeavours to procure her Liking to his Person, which if he can compass, the Lady in a little while resigns her self to him before Witnesses in a most solemn manner; at Night they go to Bed together, where the most reserv'd Virgin very tamely suffers him to do what he pleases, and the upshot is, that he obtains what he wanted without having ever ask'd for it. (I, 72–73)

In most of Mandeville's "Remarks" there is a similar progression from abstract principle to increasingly provocative illustration. There is nothing very controversial, for example, about Mandeville's opening endorsement in "Remark O" of the truism that actions speak louder than words. Characteristically, Mandeville starts by dramatizing the point with a sprightly example: "*John* never cuts any Pudding, but just enough that you can't say he took none; this little Bit, after much chomping and chewing you see goes down with him like chopp'd Hay; after that he falls upon the Beef with a voracious Appetite, and crams himself up to his Throat. Is it not provoking to hear *John* cry every Day that Pudding is all his Delight, and that he don't value the Beef of a Farthing?" (I, 151–52).

But, following this broadly applicable vignette (and after cheerfully citing himself as one who finds it easier to profess high ideals than to practice them), Mandeville turns his attention to the specific—and touchy—subject of clerical hypocrisy. At first Mandeville limits himself to Roman Catholic examples, rehearsing the stories (so reassuringly familiar to his mostly Protestant audience) of secret debauchery among the members of religious orders ostensibly dedicated to poverty and self-mortification. Before his readers can become too self-righteously edified, however, Mandeville has launched into a much fuller and more circumstantial indictment of the "Reverend Divines of all Sects, even of the most Reformed Churches in all Countries" (I, 154). These are the men, says Mandeville, who endlessly lecture their congregations on the spiritual benefits of self-denial and then brazenly demand for themselves "convenient Houses, handsome Furniture, good Fires in Winter, pleasant Gardens in Summer, neat Clothes, and Money enough to bring up their Children; Precendency in all Companies, Respect from every body, and then as much Religion as you please" (I, 155).

From this broadside covering Protestant clergymen "of all Sects," Mandeville then narrows his sights more particularly on Church of England ministers. Citing the apologetics of Anglicans like Dr. John Eachard (author of *Grounds & Occasions of the Contempt of the Clergy and Religion Enquired into,* 1670), Mandeville scoffs at the common assertion that English clergymen value material luxuries not for their own sakes, but only as symbols appropriate to the dignity of the cloth:

He that harangues on the Contempt of Riches, and the Vanity of Earthly Enjoyments, in a rusty threadbare Gown, because he has no other, and would wear his old greasy Hat no longer if any body would give him a better; that drinks Small-beer at Home with a heavy Countenance, but leaps at a Glass of Wine if he can catch it Abroad; that with little Appetite feeds upon his own coarse Mess, but falls to greedily where he can please his Palate, and expresses an uncommon Joy at an Invitation to a splendid Dinner: 'Tis he that is despised, not because he is Poor, but because he knows not how to be so with that Content and Resignation which he preaches to others, and so discovers his Inclinations to be contrary to his Doctrine (I, 157).

To an imaginary "charitable young Gentlewoman" who might object that the hardships of clerical poverty fall likewise upon innocent wives and children, Mandeville's answer is brisk and to the point: unless he has outside income, a person whose benefice is poor has no business marrying. "Marriage is lawful, and so is a Coach; but what is that to People that have not Money enough to keep one?" (I, 160).

The resentment that pious Anglicans (not to mention their ministers) would by now have felt over so unceremonious

a treatment of men in Holy Orders could only have been
increased by the sly precision of Mandeville's parting shot:

A Man has as much Opportunity to practice Temperance, that has
but one Dish at a Meal, as he that is constantly serv'd with three
Courses and a dozen Dishes in each: One may exercise as much
Patience, and be as full of Self-denial on a few Flocks, without Cur-
tains or Tester, as in a Velvet Bed that is Sixteen Foot high.... therefore I shall never believe, but that an indifferent Skuller, if he was
entrusted with it, might carry all the Learning and Religion that one
Man can contain, as well as a Barge with Six Oars, especially if it
was but to cross from *Lambeth* to *Westminster;* or that Humility
is so ponderous a Virtue, that it requires six Horses to draw it. (I,
162–63)

From the specific references to Lambeth, Westminster, and
a carriage drawn by six horses, it would have been amply
clear to Mandeville's contemporaries that the target of these
seemingly general remarks was no less a figure than the
Archbishop of Canterbury. Here, as in so much of the *Fable
of the Bees*, Mandeville has all but ensured a heated response
from a great many readers. To begin a line of argument with
the assertion that men seldom live up to their professed ideals
is merely to reaffirm a generality everyone readily accepts.
But to conclude—after a series of ever more pointed
illustrations—that the Archbishop of Canterbury in particular
exemplifies hypocrisy is a highly effective, if obvious, way
of denying an Anglican audience the luxury of indifference.
   Even in those parts of the work in which he limits himself
to general theory, Mandeville's penchant for the concrete and
dramatic helps to produce a satirically cutting edge. A case
in point is the "Enquiry into the Origin of Moral Virtue" which
first appeared in the 1714 edition of the *Fable of the Bees*.
In this brief essay Mandeville undertakes to explain how so
inveterately selfish a creature as man was originally persuaded
to accept, however imperfectly, the constraints of a moral code
based on self-denial. In the state of nature, as Mandeville
depicts it, man was devoid of all moral concepts and bent
only on satisfying his own savage appetites. Since force alone
could not make man socially tractable, civilization became
possible only after certain "Lawgivers and other wise Men"
hit upon an effective psychological means of influencing men

to curb their selfish impulses. Perceiving that man's enormous vanity made him particularly susceptible to flattery, these law-givers set out to convince men "how unbecoming it was the Dignity of such sublime Creatures to be sollicitous about gratifying those Appetites, which they had in common with Brutes" (I, 43). By means of such shrewdly chosen arguments, moral and intellectual superiority became identified with self-denial; thereafter, the standards of honor and shame—tirelessly invoked by "the skilful Management of wary Politicians"—worked as powerful inducements for public spirit and cooperation.

Predictably, Mandeville's critics found this version of the genesis of morality offensive, even though in passing he had piously conceded that the moral code thus engendered became "perfect" only with the advent of Christianity. What irritated Mandeville's commentators, however, was not so much the logical substance of his ideas as the unedifying terms in which he had expressed them. For, as Arthur Lovejoy has shown, if we take the trouble to recast Mandeville's basic arguments into the soothing abstractions of philosophic language, they lose at once most of their shock value and all of their comic vitality:

Leave out the "wary politicians," the innuendoes, the ironic by-play, and all the accessories which Mandeville introduced to amuse or horrify his readers, and his general thesis, in the essay [on the "Origin of Moral Virtue"], comes down to this; that approbativeness and the desire for self-esteem and the aversion from their opposites are the initial and the principal subjective sources, the inner and distinctively human appetencies, from which, in fact, the kind of conduct usually recognized as moral arises; that these are the affective components of human nature through which the interests of other men and the moral standards of a society get their hold upon the conduct of the individual. And *this* was no novelty and, so expressed, was hardly a paradox. It had... been said by more than one before Mande-ville....[8]

II   *Mandeville as a Cultural Evolutionist*

Though it is true, as Lovejoy indicates, that Mandeville's central thesis in the "Origin of Moral Virtue" is not original with him, it should be pointed out that the essay does show an awareness, remarkable for its time, of the evolutionary development of cultural patterns. Read as history, Mandeville's account of guileful leaders and naive savages is sufficiently absurd; but read as a parable, in which a gradual historic process is allegorized for dramatic effect, the essay reveals what Kaye has called Mandeville's "precocious feeling for evolution" (I, lxv).

For the benefit of literal-minded readers who mistakenly assumed that he thought virtue had been invented overnight by a particular set of men, Mandeville later took pains to make his position clear. In the *Enquiry into the Origin of Honour* (1732), written largely to correct the misconceptions of his critics, Mandeville's spokesman, Cleomenes, is asked: "But, how are you sure, that this [the concept of honor] was the Work of Moralists and Politicians, as you seem to insinuate?" Cleomenes replies:

I give those names promiscuously to All that, having studied Human Nature, have endeavour'd to civilize Men, and render them more and more tractable, either for the Ease of Governours and Magistrates, or else for the Temporal Happiness of Society in general. I think of all Inventions of this sort... that they are the joint Labour of Many. Human Wisdom is the Child of Time. It was not the Contrivance of one Man, nor could it have been the Business of a few Years, to establish a Notion, by which a rational Creature is kept in Awe for Fear of it Self, and an Idol is set up, that shall be its own Worshipper.[9]

Passages like this (and there are others similar to it in the *Fable of the Bees*[10]) led Sterling Lamprecht to conclude that Mandeville was "far ahead of the bulk of his contemporaries in insight into the gradual emergence through long historic changes of the culture most men take for granted as inevitable and normal."[11]

III   *The Charity-School Essay*

For all the abrasiveness of its manner and expression, the *Fable of the Bees* of 1714 seems at first to have attracted no more attention than the original *Grumbling Hive* of 1705. However, when Mandeville reissued the work in 1723, expanding the "Remarks" and adding two essays ("On Charity and Charity-Schools" and "A Search into the Nature of Society"), the response—in the form of a furious counter-attack—came almost at once; and it continued scarcely abated throughout most of the eighteenth century. Before the critics were through, they were to subject the entire book to indignant appraisal; but the immediate occasion and object of their anger was the charity school essay. More than any other single element in the *Fable of the Bees* this supremely unsentimental essay helped to earn Mandeville his contemporary reputation as the enemy of virtue, and to this day his admirers have usually found it easier to explain than to endorse the chilling assumptions upon which the essay is based.

Though free schools catering to the poor were not unknown in England prior to the eighteenth century, they had always been so few in number that the vast majority of lower-class children could expect to receive no formal education whatever. With the aim of remedying this situation the Society for Promoting Christian Knowledge organized a movement in 1699 with the avowed objective of establishing a charity school for the poor in every parish in Britain. Enthusiastically endorsed by both the Anglican and Non-Conformist clergy, the idea spread rapidly, and by the time Mandeville wrote his essay, several hundred such schools already existed—some endowed by individual philanthropists, but most supported and controlled by small contributors "of the middling sort" united in joint stock companies. Since the sponsors of charity schools were usually concerned with improving the poor morally rather than intellectually, instruction in most schools was limited to reading the Bible and to learning the catechism, though occasionally simple arithmetic was also taught.[12] The charity school movement in its early years had its detractors; but, for the most part, their criticism was guarded and oblique, since few men cared to go on record as enemies of Christian benevolence. The threat of public opprobrium, however, proved no deterrent to Mandeville; and his attack, when it came, was nothing if not direct.

Mandeville opens his essay by defining charity as "that Virtue by which part of that sincere Love we have for our selves is transferr'd pure and unmix'd to others ... " (I, 253). The operative words for Mandeville are "pure and unmix'd," for, as he goes on to explain, no action can be considered genuinely charitable unless (as is almost never the case) it is entirely untainted by any selfish desire to think well of oneself or to win the good opinion of others. Much more common than real charity (and frequently mistaken for it) is pity, that emotion which prompts us to alleviate the visible distress of others. That pity is an amiable quality, Mandeville readily concedes; but he is unwilling to call it a virtue, since it derives ultimately from a self-indulgent wish to spare ourselves the mental anguish of unpleasant sights and feelings. As Mandeville observes, " . . . thousands give Money to Beggars from the same Motive as they pay their Corn-cutter, to walk easy" (I, 259). Morally speaking, then, philanthropy is simply a form of human egotism—another of those private vices which lead to incidental public benefits—in this case, the necessary support of those unable to help themselves. When charity becomes "too extensive" and promiscuous, however, its bad effects very soon outweigh the good, as his examination of the charity school movement shows.

In any complex society, says Mandeville, there is a vast and irreducible amount of drudgery and hard physical labor that must be performed if commerce, agriculture, and the arts are to flourish. All experience shows that such unpleasant but crucial work will be done only by those who have no choice in the matter. In a society where slavery is disallowed, it is only dire personal need that will ever induce large numbers of people to spend their lives toiling at lowly tasks. To lavish charity on the poor, therefore, is to remove their sole incentive for working at all; and the inevitable result of such ill-advised benevolence is "but to breed Drones and destroy Industry" (I, 267). Furthermore, if laborers are to remain tractable and diligent, they must be psychologically reconciled to their humble stations in life; and to this end prudence requires they be kept ignorant and benighted as well as poor. With this last point, Mandeville comes to the crux of his case against the charity schools; for he contends that such schools, by fostering unrealistic ambitions and desires, effectively ruin their pupils for the laborious roles to which society has assigned them.

The usual arguments offered in favor of charity schools Mandeville finds unconvincing. That the schools provide useful moral and religious training is no doubt true; but the same instruction, he points out, could be adequately conveyed in Sunday Schools, especially if attendance were made compulsory for the poor. Proponents of charity schools likewise boast that their students learn good manners and civility. Mandeville is skeptical of this claim, but finds it irrelevant, even if correct. For "It is not Compliments we want of them, but their Work and Assiduity" (I, 270). Mandeville also gives short shrift to those who believe that charity schools help to reduce crime. It is much more probable, he says, that charity school alumni—having been rendered unfit for a life of honest hard work —will be naturally tempted to crime, in which activity they will be able to put into practical use the skills their education has afforded them. In sum, then, the charity schools have very little to recommend them; and only the hypocritical cant of their supporters, coupled with "an unreasonable Vein of Petty Reverence for the Poor" (I, 311), has made them popular.

The immediate notoriety which Mandeville's "Essay on Charity and Charity-Schools" achieved is not hard to understand. With his usual bluntness, he has disdained to hide behind the sort of euphemism and evasion that might have softened the harsh outlines of his position. The essay is characterized throughout by a lofty mercantilist contempt for the conventional moral pieties that interfere with the effective management of the poor. He seems to take a fierce pleasure in the very ruthlessness of his stand; for nothing suggests that he feels either reluctant or apologetic about consigning most of mankind to lives of hopeless drudgery. Nor does he try, like some of his contemporaries, to place the responsibility upon God; in Mandeville's argument, pure economic expediency—not God's mysterious plan—justifies keeping the lower orders in a perpetual state of poverty and ignorance.[13]

Without denying the brutality of Mandeville's position, it is worth pointing out that his callousness has frequently been exaggerated by his opponents. His compassion for the poor may be less than overwhelming, but it is not totally lacking. He does not wish to see anyone denied the means of sustenance, and he specifies that "Young Children without Parents, Old Age without Support, and all that are disabled from Working, ought to be taken care of with Tenderness and Alacrity" (I, 267). Moreover, there is a certain bleak validity in his contention that the poor suffer less when resigned to hard reality than when they have been led to entertain expectations that contemporary society is quite unprepared to satisfy:

Men who are to remain and end their Days in a Laborious, Tiresome and Painful Station of Life, the sooner they are put upon it at first, the more patiently they'll submit to it for ever after. Hard Labour and the coarsest Diet are a proper Punishment to several kinds of Malefactors, but to impose either on those that have not been used and brought up to both is the greatest Cruelty, when there is no Crime you can charge them with. (I, 288–89)

Though such admittedly meager concessions to humanitarianism hardly clear Mandeville of the charge of brutality, we should remember that his attitude toward the poor differs from the dominant opinion of the day mostly in outspokenness. Had Mandeville expressed himself in generalities or had he added to his argument the customary sugarcoating of noble sentiment, his critics might have been hard put to find cause for complaint, since his essay does little more than state with absolute candor and in detail what was already widely accepted in practice. The rightness of keeping the poor firmly in their place was scarcely a debatable proposition in Mandeville's time. We need not accept Mandeville's jaundiced view of their motives to recognize that even the founders of charity schools had no strong desire to improve their students's earning power; instead, the schools addressed themselves almost exclusively to religious indoctrination of the sort hopefully calculated to promote resignation and obedience. As a modern historian of the movement has conceded, "The charity schools came into being chiefly . . . to *condition* the children for their primary duty in life as hewers of wood and drawers of water."[14] Thus Mandeville's argument with the advocates of charity schools really came down to a question of means rather than ends; and his basic position, albeit gratingly expressed, was anything but exceptional for the age.[15]

IV   The Attack on Shaftesbury

Mandeville's final addition to the 1723 *Fable of the Bees* was the "Search into the Nature of Society," an essay in which he repeats with additional illustrations his central thesis concerning the social and economic utility of men's moral imperfections. The "Search" is significant in that it contains Mandeville's first, full-scale attack upon the Third Earl of Shaftesbury whose optimistic philosophy furnished so natural a foil to Mandeville's skepticism. Though Shaftesbury's *Charac-*

teristicks first appeared in 1711, Mandeville had perhaps not yet read the book when he prepared the 1714 *Fable of the Bees* for the press. At any rate, there is no direct reference to Shaftesbury in the earlier edition of the *Fable* or in any of Mandeville's writings prior to the *Free Thoughts on Religion* (1720), wherein Mandeville favorably cites Shaftesbury's sentiments of religious toleration and calls him "one of the most Polite Authors of the Age."[16]

By 1723, however, Mandeville has few kind words either for Shaftesbury as a man or for his arguments that vice and virtue are everywhere and at all times the same, that men of good sense may by reason and inherent inclination determine what is morally right, and that the arts of civilization derive from man's inborn love of his kind. "The attentive Reader, who perused the foregoing part of this Book," says Mandeville in opening his essay, "will soon perceive that two Systems cannot be more opposite than his Lordship's and mine. His Notions I confess are generous and refined: They are a high Compliment to Human-kind, and capable by the help of a little Enthusiasm of Inspiring us with the most Noble Sentiments concerning the Dignity of our exalted Nature: What Pity it is that they are not true" (I, 324).

In reply to Shaftesbury's opinion that men of sound understanding will inevitably recognize and pursue identical concepts of the *"pulchrum et honestum"* (the beautiful and the virtuous), Mandeville devotes several pages to showing that men's ideas of beauty have varied so widely as to embrace diametric opposites. By the same token, "In Morals there is no greater Certainty" (I, 330); for there have been fashions in virtue as in clothing, and even such practices as polygamy and incest have been considered quite natural and virtuous by advanced societies. What makes man amenable to the constraints of civilization, then, is not his all-too-mutable perception of moral verity; still less does society result from the inherent love of one's fellow creatures which Shaftesbury claims as a universal human trait. One might better cite herrings as examples of instinctive gregariousness, says Mandeville. Men prefer company to solitude only if such company directly serves either their self-esteem or self-interest, and even then, the more intelligent the man, the more selective he is apt to be in his choice of companions. "Would not a

Man be by himself a Month . . . rather than mix with Fox-hunters . . . ?" (I, 340).

However flattering man may find it to imagine that society owes its origins and advancement to his more amiable impulses, Mandeville has no doubt that it is in fact "the Bad and Hateful Qualities of Man [which] are the first Causes that made [him] sociable beyond other Animals" (I, 344). We live, he explains, in a hostile world where no single individual can ever hope independently to satisfy (except on the most brutish level) his many needs and desires. Like Hobbes, Mandeville believes that men originally formed societies on the basis of a purely selfish recognition that by so doing they could gain in security and comfort. In the same way, technology and the arts receive their initial inspiration and continuing support from man's overriding indulgence in his own well-being and pride. Hypocrisy leads us to disguise, even from ourselves, how utterly self-absorbed we are; but if man were really as benign as Shaftesbury would have it, says Mandeville, society could never advance beyond a static pastoralism. Having thus come back to the basic theme of his book, Mandeville concludes the "Search" by reaffirming his conviction that the "Wealth, the Glory and worldly Greatness of Nations" are the happy collective by-products of such morally reprehensible individuals as "the sensual Courtier . . . ; the Fickle Strumpet . . . ; the haughty Dutchess . . . ; the profuse Rake and [the] lavish Heir . . . " (I, 355).

What is perhaps most notable about Mandeville's attack on Shaftesbury is the insultingly *ad hominem* approach he takes toward his opponent. For in the "Search" Mandeville does not try to hide or soften his opinion that the optimism of the *Characteristicks* is a direct reflection of its author's sheltered life—a life which in itself, Mandeville suggests, shows a conspicuous lack of that zeal for public welfare Shaftesbury celebrates in his writings. Thus, early in the essay Mandeville offers to illustrate the ways in which, "for want of duly examining himself," a man may easily remain ignorant of his own real motives. To this end, Mandeville describes "a Person of Quality of Parts and Erudition, one every way resembling the Author of the Characteristicks himself":

A Man that has been brought up in Ease and Affluence, if he is of a Quiet Indolent Nature, learns to shun every thing that is troub-

lesome, and chooses to curb his Passions, more because of the Inconveniences that arise from the eager pursuit after Pleasure ... than
any dislike he has to sensual Enjoyments; and it is possible, that
a Person Educated under a great Philosopher, who was a mild and
good-natured as well as able Tutor, may in such happy Circumstances
have a better Opinion of his inward State than it really deserves,
and believe himself Virtuous, because his Passions lie dormant. He
may form fine Notions of the Social Virtues, and the Contempt of
Death, write well of them in his Closet, and talk Eloquently of them
in Company, but you shall never catch him fighting for his Country,
or labouring to retrieve any National Losses.... (I, 331–32)

The references to instruction from "a great Philosopher"
(Locke had served as Shaftesbury's tutor) and to a life spent
in scholarly seclusion point up the resemblance to Shaftesbury,
as does the unequivocal listing in the original index—almost
certainly composed by Mandeville himself—wherein the
above passage is cited under "*Shaftesbury* ... Refuted by his
own Character..." (I, 378). It is a measure of Mandeville's
scorn that he prefers to attribute Shaftesbury's life as a recluse
to social indifference rather than to the chronic poor health
that had led to that author's death in 1713 at the age of forty-two.

In the final paragraph of the "Search into the Nature of
Society" Mandeville bids farewell to his readers, hoping they
have found some diversion in a work largely composed, he
explains, for its author's private amusement. Satisfied that he
has amply demonstrated how "Private Vices by the dextrous
Management of a skilful Politician may be turned into Publick
Benefits" (I, 369), Mandeville seems to have felt that his *Fable
of the Bees* had in 1723 reached its final form. No doubt he
hoped and expected that this augmented version of his book
would attract more attention than its neglected predecessors,
but he could hardly have foreseen the full extent of a public
response that was to oblige him to devote the greater part
of his remaining literary career to the defense and embellishment of the already sizeable structure he had raised upon
the modest foundations of the *Grumbling Hive.*

V *Response to the* Fable

In the "Essay on Charity and Charity-Schools" Mandeville
had calmly predicted that his book would be denounced and
its author characterized as "an Uncharitable, Hard-hearted and

Inhuman, if not a Wicked, Profane, and Atheistical Wretch"
(I, 269). In this forecast, as in so much else, Mandeville proved
to be uncomfortably accurate; for, within a few weeks of the
book's publication, expressions of shocked indignation began
to be heard from the press, the pulpit, and (more ominously)
from the Grand Jury of Middlesex County. Typical of the
emotionalism of these early attacks were the Grand Jury's presentment and the "Letter to Lord C."—both of which Mandeville considered so little damaging that he included them
verbatim in all later editions of the *Fable*.

In the "Presentment of the Grand Jury of Middlesex County"
(published in the *Evening Post* on July 11), the *Fable of the
Bees* is charged in conjunction with the letters of "Cato," which
had appeared that spring in the *British Journal*.[17] The Grand
Jury, after expressing concern lest the continued publication
of "flagrant Impieties" provoke divine retribution, complains
that the works in question have denied the Trinity, questioned
God's providence, slandered the clergy, decried the teaching
of Christianity, and insidiously recommended "all kinds of
Vices, as being necessary to Publick Welfare" (I, 385). Though
"Cato's" letters and the *Fable* are declared collectively guilty
of all five offenses, it is obvious that the advocacy of vice
is more particularly ascribed to Mandeville, whose "strained
Apologies" and "forced Encomiums" of brothels (in "Remark
H") are pointedly cited in evidence.

The sense of moral outrage which informs the Grand Jury's
presentment is somewhat muted by the quasi-legalistic language employed. However, the anonymous author of the
"Letter to the Right Honourable Lord C." (which first appeared
in the *London Journal* on July 27) labored under no such
restraints. Like the Grand Jury, the author of the "Letter"
couples Mandeville with "Cato," and denounces both as men
"who have not only inveighed against the *National* Profession
and Exercise of Religion; and endeavour'd, with Bitterness
and Dexterity, to render it *Odious* and *Contemptible*, but are
sollicitous to hinder *Multitudes* of the Natives of this Island
from having the very *Seeds* of *Religion* sown among them
with Advantage" (I, 391).

More an angry diatribe than a reasoned refutation, the
"Letter" concentrates most of its rambling fury on the charity
school issue. "Cato" (whom the author of the "Letter" feels

should more properly be called "Cataline") bears the brunt of the attack; but, toward the end, the "profligate Author of the *Fable*" is singled out for his sinister attempts "to tear up the very Foundations of *Moral Virtue,* and establish *Vice* in its Room" (I, 397).

Unwilling to let silence be construed as an admission of guilt, Mandeville published in the *London Journal* on August 10 a brief "Vindication of the *Fable of the Bees,* from the Aspersions Contain'd in a Presentment of the Grand Jury of *Middlesex,* And An Abusive Letter to Lord *C.*" In studied contrast to the sputtering indignation of his critics, Mandeville preserves a gentlemanly composure; he professes himself more surprised than angry that his intentions should have been so misunderstood. His book, he explains, was expressly written "for the Entertainment of People of Knowledge and Education" (I, 404), those sophisticated enough to recognize the difference between an author who *describes* Vice and one who *advocates* it. As Mandeville points out (quoting his own words from "Remark T"): " ... *if I have shewn the Way to worldly Greatness, I have always without Hesitation preferr'd the Road that leads to Virtue"* (I, 407).

Clearly, says Mandeville, the charity school issue has most provoked his critics and inspired them to misrepresent his entire book. Such misrepresentation he does not deign to answer, other than by issuing a categorical denial that his *Fable* contains "the least Tittle of Blasphemy or Profaneness, or any thing tending to Immorality or the Corruption of Manners" (I, 412). Should he ever be convinced that such was not the case, he asserts in a closing flourish, he will publicly burn his book and humbly beg the nation's pardon.

Shortly after its publication in the *London Journal,* Mandeville's "Vindication" (together with the Grand Jury's presentment and the "Letter to Lord *C.*") was issued as a six-penny pamphlet which subsequently became a part of the *Fable.* But Mandeville's critics were not to be so easily silenced, and in the next few years the popgun attacks of the newspapers began to be augmented by the heavier artillery of such tracts as William Law's *Remarks upon a late Book, Entituled, the Fable of the Bees* (1724), Richard Fiddes's *General Treatise of Morality . . . With a Preface in Answer to Two Essays lately Published in the Fable of the Bees* (1724), John Dennis's *Vice and Luxury Publick Mischiefs* (1724), and George Bluet's *Enquiry . . . In which the Pleas Offered by the Author of the Fable of the Bees . . . are considered* (1725).[18] Aside from reissuing his "Vindication," Mandeville did not at first try to answer these and the other *"manifold Clamours"* (II, 3) against him. In late 1728, however, Mandeville (carefully explaining that he saw no need to modify his ideas but only wished to clarify them) came out with the *Fable of the Bees,* Part II, and thus completed the work as we have it today.

VI   *The Dialogues of Part II of the* Fable.

For Part II of the *Fable,* Mandeville turned to the literary form whose informality of manner and structure so well suited his talents, the dialogue.[19] In his preface he explains his choice by commending the dialogue as a mode of writing in which *"Things . . . look, as if they were acted, rather than told"* (II, 8); and, indeed, he claims the playwright's privilege of introducing each of his major actors with a brief character sketch. For *" . . . there is a Satisfaction, I think, in knowing ones Company; and when I am to converse with People for a considerable time, I desire to be well acquainted with them, and the sooner the better"* (II, 10). Aside from the somewhat faceless Fulvia, who makes a brief appearance in the First Dialogue, the *dramatis personae* consist of Horatio and Cleomenes; and to these two (and especially the latter) he devotes his attention.

Horatio, we learn, is a member of the *beau monde,* well-versed in the Classics, and in general, better informed *"than is usual for People of Quality, that are born to great Estates"* (II, 16). Himself a man of superior morality and strict honor, he is skeptical of the sincerity of clergymen; and he subscribes to the sentiment (which Mandeville professes to abhor) that "Priests of all Religions are the same" (II, 16). Horatio's generosity of spirit and his willingness to think well of mankind—clergymen excepted—have made him an admirer of Shaftesbury's works, in consequence of which he has conceived a dislike (based exclusively on hearsay) of the *Fable of the Bees* and its supposedly pernicious doctrines. His relationship to Cleomenes, as it emerges in the course of their conversations, is not that of humble disciple but that of an initially reluctant convert who surrenders his Shaftesburian benevolence only after he has been gradually convinced that it is rationally untenable.

Cleomenes, whose opinions Mandeville admits stand for his own, is a man of wide-ranging knowledge and interests. Originally, his viewpoint had been much like that of Horatio; but, on the basis of his own observation and a careful reading of the *Fable of the Bees* (whose author he refers to as "my Friend"), Cleomenes has become a confirmed Mandevillean. Since he is *"fully persuaded, not only of the Veracity of the Christian Religion, but likewise of the Severity of its Precepts"* (II, 17), he—with great regret, but with unflinching honesty—recognizes in himself and others the pervasive symptoms of self-love. Thus, though he is a man of unusually scrupulous moral behavior, Cleomenes *"would often complain that he was not possess'd of one Christian Virtue, and found fault with his own Actions, that had all the Appearances of Goodness, because he was conscious, he said, that they were perform'd from a wrong Principle"* (II, 18). Despite his strict concept of virtue, he deplores *"Rigorists of all Sorts"* (II, 18); for he suspects their motives and, in any case, is too much of a realist to expect that that man will ever reform. He strives, accordingly, not to change others but to instill in them the same honest self-awareness he himself has achieved with Mandeville's help.

In these introductory character sketches Mandeville has sought to endow his interlocutors with just enough individuality to make for verisimilitude but not so much as to interfere with their primary function as representative figures. Hence, he has preferred not to assign them descriptive or allegorical names, and he also insists that both characters, though fictional, are portraits faithfully drawn from life. Aside from their differing viewpoints, however, Horatio and Cleomenes are not sharply distinguishable dramatic personalities. Neither displays any noticeable idiosyncracies, and both speak throughout with equally accomplished eloquence, politeness, and wit. Defined, as they are, by their opinions, the two speakers inevitably tend to take on a sameness of voice as, with each new stage in their discussion, Horatio's conversion becomes more complete.

So thoroughly does Cleomenes carry the day that Donald Davie has described Horatio as "a man of straw" whose counterarguments consist of little more than some "perfunctory huffing and puffing in the first two dialogues."[20] But such a description exaggerates Horatio's docility; he always comes

around in the end, and often as not he accompanies his agreement with generous compliments to Cleomenes's per-
suasiveness. However, as mentioned above, his surrender is
piecemeal—more a series of strategic retreats under fire than
a token resistance followed by sudden collapse. Nor, in fact,
is his overall capitulation unqualified; for, in addition to his
obvious role as a sounding board, Horatio is sometimes used
to express opinions with which Mandeville agrees but which
for politic reasons he prefers not to place in the mouth of
his avowed spokesman, Cleomenes.

This latter technique was one which Mandeville had already
employed seventeen years earlier in the *Treatise of the
Hypochondriack and Hysterick Passions*. As we observed,
Mandeville—wishing to attack apothecaries, but thinking it
unwise to do so directly—had Misomedon deliver a vehement
denunciation, from which Philopirio (Mandeville's spokesman
in most of the work) politely demurs. In order to pave the
way for an analogous use of his speakers in Part II of the
Fable, Mandeville makes the prefactory announcement:

As it is supposed, that Cleomenes *is my Friend, and speaks my
Sentiments, so it is but Justice, that every Thing which he advances
should be look'd upon and consider'd as my own; but no Man in
his Senses would think, that I ought to be equally responsible for
every Thing that* Horatio *says, who is his Antagonist. If ever he
offers any thing that savours of Libertinism, or is otherwise excep-
tionable, which* Cleomenes *does not reprove him for in the best
and most serious Manner, or to which he gives not the most satisfactory and convincing Answer that can be made, I am to blame, otherwise not.* (II, 21–22)

By means of this prudent disclaimer, Mandeville hopes to
disassociate himself from certain of the overtly skeptical religious sentiments he has assigned to Horatio. For not only
is Horatio used to express Mandeville's anticlericalism, but,
at several crucial points in the dialogue, he—in the face of
Cleomenes's pious objections—proves willing to recognize
and accept some of the more dangerously unorthodox implications of Mandeville's philosophy. Thus, in the sixth dialogue,
after Cleomenes has ridiculed the logical absurdities and child-
ish myths of pagan religions, Horatio pointedly remarks: "You
reason very clearly, and with great Freedom, against all

heathen Superstition, and never suffer yourself to be imposed upon by any Fraud from that Quarter; but when you meet with any thing belonging to the *Jewish* or Christian Religion, you are as credulous as any of the Vulgar.... A Man that contentedly swallows every thing that is said of *Noah* and his Ark, ought not to laugh at the Story of *Deucalion* and *Pyrrha"* (II, 307). To this objection, as to similar ones, Cleomenes rather lamely responds with the uncharacteristically humble admission that, while he cannot pretend to understand the mysteries of Christianity, he nevertheless accepts them without reservation.[21]

VII   *The Tone of Part II*

In general, Mandeville's approach in Part II of the *Fable of the Bees* is far less deliberately provocative than had been the case in Part I. Mandeville does not becomes defensive or apologetic; the dominant tenor in Part II is one of good-humored explication rather than one of aggressive assertion. To a large extent, this more ingratiating tone is a natural concomitant of the dialogue form itself, at least as Mandeville conceives it. For, in a conversation between two gentlemen, decorum, if nothing else, precludes the kind of satiric abrasiveness Mandeville had earlier favored. The proper qualities of "what I call good Company" had already been made clear by Mandeville in the "Search into the Nature of Society":

There is nothing said in it that is not either instructive or diverting to a Man of Sense. It is possible [the speakers] may not always be of the same Opinion, but there can be no contest between any but who shall yield first to the other he differs from. One only speaks at a time, and no louder than to be plainly understood by him who sits farthest off. The greatest Pleasure aimed at by every one of them is to have the Satisfaction of Pleasing others, which they all practically know may as effectually be done by hearkning with Attention and an approving Countenance, as if we said very good things our selves. (I, 339–40)

It is as exemplars of this polite ideal that Horatio and Cleomenes carry on their discussions.

Since part of Mandeville's strategy is to maintain that most of the published complaints against the *Fable* are unworthy of serious notice, it is not surprising to find that Cleomenes devotes relatively little time to overt rebuttal of criticism.

Instead, he acts on the assumption that Mandeville's philosophy, honestly presented, is its own best justification; and, accordingly, he seldom adopts a defensive posture. There is, however, a major exception to Mandeville's studied indifference toward his critics, for he is anything but Olympian toward the charges leveled against the moral and religious character of his doctrines. Cleomenes repeatedly denies the *Fable*'s alleged advocacy of vice and irreligion, often as not supporting his denial with appropriately pious quotations from Part I. Likewise, Mandeville has Cleomenes spend several pages addressing himself to the charges of cruelty that were elicited by the charity school essay.

It is reflective of the general tone of Part II that in this latter instance Mandeville restates his case in terms appreciably less jarring than those he had originally used. Thus Cleomenes makes it clear that he is not unwilling to see the poor better themselves so long as that betterment is based upon personal effort and ability, rather than on the ill-advised benevolence "of perhaps well-meaning People" (II, 353). Here, as in the rest of Part II, Mandeville has not significantly revised his earlier position; he has, however, chosen to include the sort of softening qualification and nuance that in Part I he had usually left unstated or underplayed.

Another case in point is the way in which Mandeville elaborates upon the views he had first put forth in the "Enquiry into the Origin of Moral Virtue." In that essay, it will be remembered, Mandeville had pointed out that a necessary precondition for civilized society was that men be somehow induced to place the public good above their private interest. The most effective means to that end was an appeal to man's vanity, and so "skilful Politicians" in primitive times had flattered their followers with pleasing fictions about human dignity, altruism, and self-denial; and to such lowly origins may be traced our ideas of moral virtue. This argument—in which virtue appears as a purely human invention formulated by a handful of cunning men—had attracted sharp criticism, both for its impiety and its historical implausibility.

In Part II of the *Fable*, Cleomenes, without specifically acknowledging these criticisms, nevertheless undertakes to answer them by amplifying the original point. Cleomenes reaffirms the mundane beginnings of "virtue," but he also stresses sentiments that Mandeville had left muted in the "Essay." We now learn that it was God Himself who, in His generosity, arranged matters so that primitive man could anticipate (albeit imperfectly) those divine truths which would later be endorsed by Revelation. Nor was the discovery of moral virtue the work of a few clever men or a single age, as the allegorical phraseology of the "Essay" had implied. Instead, it was a slow evolutionary process in which the initially crude perceptions of moral behavior were gradually refined by the philosophers and statesmen of succeeding eras.

VIII   *The Origin of Language*

As we noted earlier, Mandeville's awareness of the evolutionary nature of culture is unusual for his age. At a time when the literal accuracy of the Bible was beyond public question, there were few historians willing to accept so unscriptural a concept.[22] To allay such misgivings, Mandeville is at some pains to demonstrate that his own evolutionary interpretations of the uncertain past do not clash with biblical authority. Protectively flanked by such denials of unorthodoxy (and by his new propensity for detecting God's supervisory hand in all human affairs), Mandeville advances a surprisingly modern view of man's prehistory and cultural beginnings, particularly on the subject of the origins and development of language, in Part II of the *Fable*.

Most of Mandeville's contemporaries thought of language not as a human invention but as a full-blown gift from God to Adam and Eve. Even those few who regarded speech as the creation of man were committed to a biblical chronology that seemingly did not allow for any long period of gradual development. Mandeville surmounts this difficulty by conceding that Adam and Eve *were* taught language all at once and by direct inspiration. Among their widely dispersed descendants, however, there were some—brutalized by postdeluvian wars and calamities unreported in scripture—who rapidly sank to a state of nature in which the very power of speech was lost. With the slow passage of time, Mandeville says, all such groups managed to recover the art of language, after which some developed civilized societies, while others (from whom today's savages derive) remained static.

Having thus cleared the ground, Mandeville is free to explain the circumstances under which primitive man invented speech. At first, Cleomenes tells Horatio, men in the wild state—having few ideas and only the most elementary desires—we able to express themselves adequately through gestures and a few animal noises to indicate rage, fear, and other such basic emotions. But when a "wild Pair" had

lived together for many Years, it is very probable, that for the Things they were most conversant with they would find out Sounds, to stir up in each other the Idea's of such Things, when they were out of sight; these Sounds they would communicate to their young ones; and the longer they lived together the greater Variety of Sounds they would invent, as well for Actions as the Things themselves: They would find that the Volubility of Tongue, and Flexibility of Voice, were much greater in their young ones, than they could remember it ever to have been in themselves: ... some of these young ones would, either by Accident or Design, make use of this superior Aptitude of the Organs at one time or other; which every Generation would still improve upon; and this must have been the Origin of all Languages, and Speech it self, that were not taught by Inspiration. (II, 287–88)

In this imaginative conjecture and in his pioneering emphasis on the "slow degrees ... and length of time" (II, 287) required for the development and diffusion of language, Mandeville significantly anticipates the philological theories of such later writers as Etienne de Condillac and Johann Herder.[23]

IX *The* Origin of Honour

By the end of the six dialogues which comprise Part II of the *Fable of the Bees,* Horatio has altogether abandoned his Shaftesburian optimism and openly acknowledged himself a convert to Mandeville's philosophy. Horatio is not, however, without questions; and the book closes with a hint of more discussions in the offing. The promise thus implied was fulfilled by Mandeville in 1732 with the publication of an *Enquiry into the Origin of Honour, and the Usefulness of Christianity in War,* in which Horatio and Cleomenes reappear to take up, as if without interruption, their earlier conversations. Mandeville proceeds on the assumption that his readers are already familiar with the personalities of his interlocutors and with the details of their previous talks, and thus,

in effect, the four dialogues of the *Origin of Honour* constitute not so much an independent work as yet another adden-
dum to Part II of the *Fable of the Bees.*[24]

The *Origin of Honour* is given over, as it were, to a specific
example within historical memory of the ways in which clever
leaders have been able to make human weaknesses contribute
to society's ends. In "Gothick" times, as Cleomenes tells
Horatio: "it was found out, that many vicious, quarrelsome,
and undaunted Men, that fear'd neither God nor Devil, were
yet often curb'd and visibly with-held by the Fear of Shame;
and likewise that this Fear of Shame might be greatly encreas'd
by an artful Education, and be made superiour even to that
of Death.... This I take to have been the Origin of
Honour...."[25]

Assured by moralists and politicians that elevated behavior
is the mark of noble persons, "illiterate Men and rude War-
riours" were soon persuaded to accept social restraints. Yet
it is significant, Cleomenes points out, that masculine hon-
or—originally formulated in broad ethical terms—soon boiled
down in practice to an all but exclusive preoccupation with
physical bravery. Toward such difficult virtues as humility,
piety, and chastity, little more than lipservice is required from
the modern man of honor; but he soon relinquishes that title
if his personal courage stays long in doubt. Hence, the near
impossibility of extirpating so palpably unchristian a practice
as dueling, wherein men of honor prefer to break the laws
of both God and state rather than to suffer the charge of coward-
ice that would inevitably attach itself to a gentleman who
ignored an affront or declined a challenge.

In national terms, war is the equivalent of dueling; and it
is obvious that an army, no less than a private man of honor,
can hardly afford to take seriously the pacifism and humility
called for in the Bible. Yet, though the best Christians are
never soldiers, it is an observable fact, says Cleomenes, that
the best soldiers are invariably "Christians." Generals long
ago discovered that an intense spirit of religiosity (as opposed
to *genuine* piety) is among the most useful attributes an army
can possess. Encouraged by military clergymen to believe that
they are doing God's work, men will fight with double zeal,
knowing that the more aggressively unchristian their behavior
is, the more they will be praised for it. The ruthless courage

of such troops becomes especially effective when, as in the
case of Oliver Cromwell, the commander shares his army's
fanaticism. But even the least religiously motivated general,
if he is wise, will see to it that his troops are at least as well
provided with chaplains as with weapons.

Though Cleomenes pretends to be saddened by the hypocrisy and self-deception through which men put a Christian
gloss on their least Christian motives, his tone more clearly
suggests that he is amused and even impressed by the
ingenuity whereby man's most dangerous impulses have been
diverted into socially useful channels. Thus, while Cleomenes
is firmly convinced that neither the fashionable code of honor
nor the practice of war can ever be reconciled to Christian
doctrine, he is no less certain that both these institutions are
of immense benefit to society—the first, as a check to noxious
behavior; the second, as a necessary aspect of national greatness and prosperity. Cleomenes's theme, then, is that which
informs all of Mandeville's thought: namely, that in man's
slow advance from barbarism, the moralists—who ask us to
deny our natures—have been far less effective than the worldly
politicians who are content to work as best they can with the
imperfect materials at hand.

In the *Origin of Honour*, as elsewhere in his works, Mandeville tries to protect himself against the charge that he is
undermining religion. Cleomenes regularly protests that he
is merely describing the principles men actually follow, rather
than those which they *should* follow and which he himself
admires. Likewise, Horatio, resuming his intermittent role as
enunciator of dangerous opinions, spells out the conclusions
that Mandeville is unwilling to assign to his own spokesman.
Thus, Cleomenes, after arguing at length on the scarcity of
genuine Christians, piously adds: "But this is no Argument
against Christianity, or the Reasonableness of its Doctrine."
To this, Horatio replies:

I don't say it is. But as the Principle of Honour, whatever Origin
it had, teaches Men to be just in all their Dealings, and true to their
Engagements, and there are considerable Numbers in every civiliz'd
Nation, who really take Delight in this Principle, and in all their
Actions are sway'd and govern'd by it, must you not allow, that such
a Principle, let it be owing to Education, to Flattery, to Pride, or

what you please, is more useful to Society than the best Doctrine in the World, which None can live up to, and but Few endeavour to follow?[26]

Cleomenes concedes that in temporal society honor is more useful than religion, but he sternly reminds Horatio that as individuals we pay a terrible price in the next life for having preferred honor to virtue in this one. But, while the latter sentiment is sufficiently orthodox, it loses much of its conviction when we recall the equanimity with which Cleomenes has admitted his own dedication to worldly values. Under the circumstances, it is hard not to agree with Horatio's summarizing remark: " ... after all, I can't see what Honour you have done to the Christian Religion, which yet you ever seem strenuously to contend for, whilst you are treating every Thing else with the utmost Freedom."[27]

At the conclusion of the *Origin of Honour*, Cleomenes and Horatio agree to meet again "in a few Days" to continue their discussions; and it seems likely, had Mandeville lived longer, that sooner or later they would have kept their date. For their dialogues had served Mandeville well by allowing him not only to expand and embellish his original arguments but to do so with a show of urbane detachment in sharp contrast to the clamorous abuse favored by most of his critics. Within a few weeks of the appearance of the *Origin of Honour*, however, Mandeville was confronted by a literary opponent more formidable than any he had hitherto faced, and—ironically enough—this new adversary chose to deliver his attack in the form of a polished, amusing dialogue.

CHAPTER 8

The Letter to Dion

THE appearance of Part II of the *Fable of the Bees* did nothing to lessen the critical attacks on Mandeville; but, as long as such attacks remained more notable for their vehemence than for their polemical effectiveness, no pressing need arose for Mandeville to issue replies. Though not all of Mandeville's early critics were as inconsiderable as he professed to find them, the usual angry emotionalism of his enemies did lend a certain plausibility to Mandeville's collective dismissal of them as mere name-callers. With the appearance in 1732 of *Alciphron, or the Minute Philosopher,* however, a new and less easily ignored opponent entered the lists. For, unlike previous anti-Mandevilleans, George Berkeley (1685 –1753) wisely surmised that ridicule would be an infinitely more telling weapon than vituperation.

In 1728, Berkeley, then Dean of Derry, had set out for Newport, Rhode Island, on what was intended as the first stage of a journey to Bermuda, where he hoped to establish a missionary college. Berkeley was to spend three years in Newport waiting (in vain, as it turned out) for his proposed college to win the backing it needed, and it was during this period of enforced idleness that he composed *Alciphron.* His avowed design, as he subsequently expressed it in the "Advertisement" to *Alciphron,* was "to consider the free-thinker in the various lights of atheist, libertine, enthusiast, scorner, critic, metaphysician, fatalist, and sceptic . . ."[1] "Free-thinker," in Berkeley's usage, becomes a classification broad enough to embrace such seemingly disparate writers as Mandeville, Shaftesbury, Matthew Tindal, Anthony Collins, and John Tillotson. However much they might disagree in their philosophical premises, all such authors (as Berkeley saw them) resembled one another in their efforts to undermine revealed religion and "to unhinge the principles of morality" (23). By calling them "minute" philosophers, Berkeley hoped to underscore both the narrowness of their vision and their propensity for diminishing whatever they dealt with.

I   *The Characters of* Alciphron *and its Attack on Mandeville*

The seven dialogues comprising *Alciphron* occur on the days of one week, during which Euphranor (a prosperous farmer) and Crito ("a neighbouring gentleman of distinguished merit and estate"—p. 32) debate the tenets of minute philosophy with Alciphron and Lysicles, both of whom are self-proclaimed free-thinkers. The conversations are reported in a letter to a friend by Dion, who attends but does not participate in the discussions. As their descriptive names suggest, Euphranor ("the cheerful man") and Crito ("the judicious man") represent between them Berkeley's viewpoint. In the give and take of the dialogues, Euphranor's unaffected piety and simple honesty are nicely augmented by Crito's learning and wit, and together they form a persuasive combination far superior to anything the opposition can offer.

Mandeville was later to complain that Berkeley, in portraying Alciphron and Lysicles, had resorted to caricature, with the result that both characters were obvious strawmen designed for easy refutation. But such a complaint, though valid enough, understandably fails to do justice to Berkeley's skill and to his shrewd instinct for the *kind* of caricature that would best serve his purpose. Had Berkeley chosen to represent his free-thinkers as satanic exemplars of evil, his attack would have differed little from the usual diatribes on the subject. Instead, he prefers to depict Alciphron and Lysicles as essentially comic figures whose fatuous personalities and transparently fallacious doctrines are meant to inspire at least as much laughter as indignation. Crito dryly understates the case when he remarks that the two men have about them "a certain air and manner which a little too visibly declare they think themselves wiser than the rest of the world" (33). In point of fact, Alciphron and Lysicles might be more accurately described as offensively cocksure in their opinions, as jauntily patronizing in their demeanor, and as ludicrously oblivious in their indifference to logical objection.

Despite the generic characteristics they share as free-thinkers, Alciphron and Lysicles remain, however, distinguishable in doctrine and, to a lesser extent, in personality. Alciphron, who prefers the Deistic or Shaftesburian system,[2] is the elder of the two; and, though he prides himself on being strictly up-to-date, he is something of a pedant, who punctuates his discourse with allusions to ancient authors. His name —literally, "strong mind," by which Berkeley intends something like "bull-headed"—suggests the blind obstinacy with which he resists rational correction. As the title character and representative of the most numerous sect of minute philosophers, Alciphron occupies the center of the stage, distinctly overshadowing his younger and less articulate friend.

In assigning a conspicuously subsidiary role to Lysicles —who is an enthusiastic Mandevillean—Berkeley tacitly suggests that he does not consider Mandeville's doctrines substantial enough to require elaborate refutation. From Berkeley's point of view, the essence (and, indeed, very nearly the entirety) of Mandeville's philosophy lies in its presumed advocacy of vice as the highest social good. Such, at any rate, is Lysicles's position; and, in presenting it, he renders both it and himself so palpably absurd as to make formal rebuttal almost superfluous. As a man of pleasure (his name means "one of loose reputation"), Lysicles endorses the *Fable of the Bees* because it furnishes him with a rationale for indulging his worst impulses.

Though Lysicles is fond of explicating that rationale, he does not (like Alciphron) relish debate. His answers to objections are brief and often pert to the point of frivolity, so much so that on one occasion the usually polite Crito sharply tells him: "If you have a mind to argue, we will argue; if you have more mind to jest, we will laugh with you" (213). Typical of Lysicles's self-revealing discourse is his remark in response to Alciphron's denunciation of the universities as "nurseries of prejudice." "For my part," says Lysicles, "I find no fault with the universities. All I know is that I had the spending [of] three hundred pounds a year in one of them, and think it the cheerfulest time of my life. As for their books and style, I had not leisure to mind them" (197).

The direction of Berkeley's attack on Mandeville suggests that his knowledge of the *Fable of the Bees* was limited to Part I; for there are no clear allusions in *Alciphron* to Part II, which did not appear until some months after Berkeley had left England for Rhode Island. It is interesting to note, however, that in *Alciphron* Berkeley employs against Shaftesbury an illustrative analogy nearly identical to one Mandeville had used in Part II of the *Fable*. In Mandeville's version, Cleomenes compares the Mandevillean viewpoint to that of a realistic Dutch painting of the Nativity, complete with a wealth of carefully observed "abject, low, pitiful, and mean" detail. The Shaftesburian viewpoint he likens to an idealized representation of the same subject; this one is done with "Pillars of the *Corinthian* Order" and with all the "low" details removed.[3] In much the same fashion (though with a different end in mind), Berkeley has Alciphron contrast two drawings —one "finished by the nice and laborious touches of a Dutch pencil, and another off-hand scratched out in the free manner of a great Italian master" (49). As a good Shaftesburian, Alciphron naturally prefers the latter, though he objects not so much to the realism of the Dutch piece as to the constricting emphasis upon method, precision, and closely studied detail.

   The attack on Mandeville is concentrated in Dialogue Two of *Alciphron*, though he is not altogether spared in the rest of the tract. Clearly, Mandeville is identifiable as part of the larger target when Berkeley charges the minute philosophers with such things as anticlericalism, intellectual arrogance, and contempt for religion. In Dialogue Two, however, Mandeville is singled out (though not by name) for individual attention when Berkeley offers a *reductio ad absurdum* of the *Fable's* doctrines concerning the social utility of vice. Like many another disciple, Lysicles is always willing to go his master one better. Ideas that Mandeville merely implies or carefully qualifies, Lysicles flatly asserts—usually in the grossest terms and frequently as a prelude to his own extravagant embellishments. The result is not so much a formal explication as a disconnected rhapsody in praise of "the beautiful and never-enough-admired connexion of vices" (68). In brief, what Lysicles has deduced from his reading of Mandeville comes down to a few simple propositions, which Crito accurately paraphrases as follows:

—that there is no God or providence: that man is as the beasts that perish: that his happiness as theirs consists in obeying animal instincts, appetites, and passions: that all stings of conscience and sense of guilt are prejudices and errors of education: that religion is a State trick: that vice is beneficial to the public: that the soul of man is corporeal, and dissolveth like a flame or vapour: that man is a machine actuated according to the laws of motion: that consequently he is no agent, or subject of guilt: that a wise man will make his own particular individual interest in this present life the rule and measure of all his actions. (107)

Such (in Berkeley's view) were Mandeville's doctrines when stripped of euphemism. During the course of the dialogue, honest Euphranor is at first astonished, then incredulous, and at length bemused at what he describes as a set of "opinions . . . so bad that no good man can endure them, and . . . arguments so weak that no wise man will admit them" (106). Lysicles is quite undisturbed by this judgment, for he airily dismisses all counterarguments—whether moral, logical, or practical—as the superstitious quibbling of unliberated minds. Since Lysicles is so palpably a fool, it is hard to take him very seriously as a monster, and accordingly Berkeley treats him and his doctrines with a comtempt made all the more devastating by the good humor with which it is conveyed.

II *Mandeville's Response*

Whatever its objective virtues or defects as an interpretation of the *Fable of the Bees*, Berkeley's *Alciphron* was clearly not a work that Mandeville could afford to ignore. Nor, by all indications, was he inclined to do so; for his reply (which appeared within a few weeks of *Alciphron)* gives ample support to Jacob Viner's contention that "Berkeley . . . more than any other critic seems to have gotten under Mandeville's skin. . . ."[4] The *Letter to Dion, Occasion'd by a Book Call'd Alciphron* largely abandons the icey hauteur with which Mandeville had answered his previous critics. Instead, in this, his final work, Mandeville writes throughout with a sense of aggrieved injury that sometimes approaches the querulous.

There is a deceptively mild tone in the opening pages of the *Letter to Dion*, for Mandeville begins by politely commending Dion as one whose "Style and whole Manner of Writing" clearly bespeak an author of "Learning, good Sense and Capacity" (1). Since Mandeville cannot believe that such a man would *knowingly* have misrepresented the truth, he will proceed on the assumption that Dion has not read the

Fable of the Bees at all, but rather (like "Thousands of...
well-meaning People"—p. 1) has innocently swallowed the
"spiteful Inferences" disseminated by the book's enemies.
Without rancor, then, and solely in the interests of truth and
his own good name, Mandeville proposes to inform Dion of
what the *Fable* actually says; and in fulfillment of this promise
Mandeville devotes a large proportion of the *Letter* to direct
quotations from the earlier work.

Mandeville's insistence that Berkeley relied on hearsay for
his knowledge of the *Fable* (a conception, incidentally, with
which at least one modern critic agrees[5] carries with it certain
rhetorical advantages. By choosing to reduce the charge from
malicious slander to simple gullibility, Mandeville ostensibly
demonstrates his own magnanimity and good will. His overt
expressions of indignation are reserved for the unnamed ca-
lumniators who have deliberately spread false versions of his
doctrines: toward Berkeley himself, Mandeville's strongest
explicit reproval takes the form of a relatively mild reminder
that one who has not himself read a book perhaps "ought
not to be so magisterial in his Censures" of it (30).

Mandeville's forebearance, however, is much more apparent
than real; and, in the process of announcing his firm belief
in Berkeley's good faith, Mandeville usually manages to suggest quite the contrary opinion. Thus, early in the *Letter*, Mandeville elaborately "excuses" Dion in terms that carry the force
of an indictment:

I find no Fault with you, Sir; for whilst a Person believes these
Accusations against me to be true, and is entirely unacquainted with
the Book they point at, it is not impossible that he might inveigh
against it without having any Mischief in his Heart. . . . A Man may
be credulous and yet well disposed; but if a Man of Sense and Pene-
tration, who had actually read the *Fable of the Bees*, and with Attention perused every Part of it, should write against it in the same strain,
as *Dion* has done in his second Dialogue, then I must confess, I
should be at a Loss, what Excuse to make for him. (3).

I can't say, that there are not several Passages in that Dialogue,
which would induce one to believe, that you had dipt into the Fable
of the Bees; but then to suppose, that upon having only dipt in it,
you would have wrote against it as you have done, would be so
injurious to your Character, the Character of an honest Man, that
I have not Patience to reason upon such an uncharitable Supposi-
tion. (5)

The greater part of the *Letter to Dion* is devoted to Mandeville's systematic consideration of the various ways in which his principles and beliefs have been distorted, falsified, and otherwise misrepresented in *Alciphron.* One by one Mandeville lists the objectionable opinions ascribed to him, and then answers each with a corrective quotation of his actual words as found in the *Fable of the Bees.* Within this documentary framework, Mandeville very effectively dramatizes the sizeable gulf between his recorded sentiments and Berkeley's transmogrification of them. As Mandeville cites each new example of how ill he has been used, his indignation grows more pronounced; and, though he continues to refrain from openly accusing Berkeley of anything worse than irresponsibility, it is clear that, by the end of the tract, we, as readers, are meant to take a much less charitable view.

If nothing more than Berkeley's accuracy as a reporter were in question, the *Letter to Dion* would be unanswerable; for it can hardly be denied that Lysicles's opinions constitute a patent travesty of Mandeville's published thought. It is Berkeley's opinion, however, that only through such a broadly interpretive approach can the genuine import of the minute philosophers be revealed, since in their writings these authors lean heavily on protective ambiguities, insincere disclaimers, and satiric obfuscations. As Euphranor puts it:

> ... methinks, it is a vain attempt for a plain man of any settled belief or principles to engage with such slippery, fugitive, changeable philosophers. It seems as if a man should stand still in the same place, while his adversary chooses and changes his situation, has full range and liberty to traverse the field, and attack him on all sides and in all shapes, from a nearer or farther distance, on horseback or on foot, in light or heavy armour, in close fight or with missive weapons. (321)

Under the circumstances, Berkeley feels it would be naive to accept at face value the public avowals of men whose most repugnant ideas take the form of pointed hints and sly innuendoes left for the reader to formulate. Accordingly, Berkeley created in Lysicles a portrait not of Mandeville but of an outspoken disciple who is not afraid to articulate all the unstated implications (as Berkeley sees them) of his master's philosophy. "Their writers are of different opinions," Crito says of the free-thinkers. "Some go farther, and explain themselves more freely than others. But the current and general notions of the sect are best learned from conversation with those who profess themselves of it"(32).

Whatever we may think of the legitimacy of Berkeley's approach, it is obviously a difficult one to counter. Mandeville has no trouble in proving that he has nowhere *proclaimed* most of the offensive ideas attributed to him, but it is almost impossible for him to demonstrate that he never *implied* them. There is really very little that Mandeville can do against such attack except issue categorical denials of any ulterior motives and reiterate that "tho' I have shewn the Way to Worldly Greatness, I have, without Hesitation, preferr'd the Road that leads to Virtue" (31).

Mandeville is fully aware of the futility of protesting his own sincerity, and even as he continues to do so, he wearily anticipates how little credence his assertions are likely to win among the skeptical:

I know, that my Enemies won't allow, that I wrote with this View; tho' I have told them before, and demonstrated, that the *Fable* of the *Bees* was a Book of exalted Morality; they refuse to believe me; their Clamours against it continue; and what I have now said in Defence of it, will be rejected, and call'd an Artifice to come off; that it is full of dangerous, wicked and Atheistical Notions, and could not have been wrote with any other Design than the Encouragement of Vice. (24)

From Dion, however, Mandeville professes to expect better treatment; and, now that the injury done him has been made apparent, he closes the *Letter to Dion* "in full Expectation, that, in what relates to me, I shall find great Alterations in your next Edition" (66). This expectation, needless to say, was not to be fulfilled; but, in the second edition of *Alciphron* (1732—it was not to achieve a third until 1752), Berkeley did take brief notice of those who, like Mandeville, had accused him of falsifying the beliefs of his opponents.[6] In a paragraph added to the original "Advertisement" Berkeley points out:

As the author hath not confined himself to write agianst books alone, so he thinks it necessary to make this declaration. It must not therefore be thought that authors are misrepresented if every notion of Alciphron or Lysicles is not found precisely in them. A gentleman in private conversation may be supposed to speak plainer than others write, to improve upon their hints, and draw conclusions from their principles. (23)

In polemical contests of the sort represented by *Alciphron* and the *Letter to Dion* there are seldom any unequivocal victors. The nature of such tracts is that they serve not so much to persuade the skeptical as to reinforce the opinions of those already convinced. Even today scholars have been unable to agree as to the relative effectiveness of the two works. *Alciphron*'s modern editor, T. E. Jessop, contends that Berkeley's summary of Mandeville's doctrines is a "not unfair" assessment of a philosophy that "tore man out of heaven and put him into the stye. I can see no reason for whitewashing Mandeville. The content and manner of his writing invite retort rather than argument. Berkeley gives both, in the most sparkling of his dialogues. Mandeville wrote a feeble reply..." (10).

Beside this comment, we may place the opinion of J. C. Maxwell, who remarks: "Berkeley never wrote anything that is less to his credit than his attack on Mandeville, and Mandeville's reply is admirably cool and good-tempered."[7] A more even-handed judgment is that of Bonamy Dobrée, who describes *Alciphron* as a "brilliant collection of dialogues," albeit one in which Berkeley "didn't play altogether fair."[8] By the same token, Dobrée, considers the *Letter to Dion* "a dignified rebuke," yet one in which "Mandeville seems here and there to flag a little...."[9] Given such divergency of views, it may perhaps suffice to point out that the greatest compliment to Berkeley's skill lies in the readiness with which the aging Mandeville recognized the challenge posed by *Alciphron*. Mandeville rose to the occasion with a characteristically vigorous and trenchant defense of his position; and, as such, the *Letter to Dion* seems an altogether appropriate finale to his long career.

When Mandeville died on January 21, 1733, only two English periodicals printed obituary remarks. In *Berington's Evening Post* (January 23) and in *Applebee's Original Weekly Journal* (January 27) there appeared the identical notice:

On Sunday Morning last died at Hackney, in the 63rd Year of his

Age, Bernard Mandeville, M.D. Author of the Fable of the Bees, of a Treatise of the Hypochondriac and Hysteric Passions and several other curious Pieces, some of which have been published in Foreign Languages. He had an extensive Genius, uncommon Wit, and Strong Judgment. He was thoroughly versed in the Learning of the Ancients, well skill'd in many Parts of Philosophy, and a curious Searcher into Human Nature; which Accomplishments rendered him a valuable and entertaining Companion, and justly procured him the Esteem of Men [of] Sense and Literature. In his Profession he was of known Benevolence and Humanity; in his private Character, a sincere Friend; and in the whole Conduct of Life, a Gentleman of great Probity and Integrity.[10]

Few of Mandeville's contemporaries, however, were willing to be quite so generous, at least in print; and the attacks on the *Fable of the Bees* did not abate with its author's death. Nor did Mandeville's notoriety long remain limited to Britain, for the *Fable* was translated into French in 1740 and into German in 1761. On the Continent (where Mandeville's *Free Thoughts on Religion* had earlier made his name known), the *Fable* elicited condemnations scarcely less vehement than those it had received in England; indeed, in France the book was at one time ordered burned by the common hangman. F. B. Kaye, who has compiled a useful chronological list of references to Mandeville's works,[11] remarks (on the basis of that list) that "the vogue of the *Fable* in England was greatest from 1723 to about 1755. From then until about 1835, it retained its celebrity, but had apparently ceased to be an active sensation."[12]

Through most of the nineteenth century and the earlier part of the twentieth, Mandeville's works, while never althogether forgotten, were not often reprinted. With the passage of time, many of his ideas—by now made familiar in different form through the writings of Adam Smith, Jeremy Bentham, and others—had come to seem less shocking, though paradoxically Mandeville's name continued to be invoked as that of an especially pernicious writer. Kaye explains Mandeville's comparative eclipse:

Generations had been trained to think of him as a sort of philosophical antichrist, and scandal was the normal association with the *Fable*. After a while the scandal became stale. When that happened, Mandeville's renown passed, for, at that date, in the public mind, nothing impelling to interest besides the now dead scandal was sufficiently associated with Mandeville to preserve him. A *succès de scandale* is never permanent. Sooner or later, if the author is to live, his fame must be built afresh on other grounds.[13]

In our own time the "other grounds" on which Mandeville's reputation rests have been several. The appearance in 1924 of Kaye's distinguished edition of the *Fable of the Bees* paved the way for Mandeville's subsequent emergence from the relative obscurity into which he had fallen, and he began at last to receive appropriate recognition for his significant contributions to social philosophy, economic thought, and psychological theory. Yet, important as these contributions are, for the general reader it will always be Mandeville's literary excellence that most strongly commends him to attention. For after two and one half centuries, Mandeville's best works remain as readable, as entertaining, and as stimulating as when he first wrote them down; and Thomas R. Edwards, Jr., does him no more than justice in calling him the author of a body of "prose that has an enduring claim as literature of a high order indeed."[14]

Notes and References

Chapter One

1. See Bernard Mandeville, *The Fable of the Bees*, ed. by F. B. Kaye, 2 vols. (Oxford, 1957), I, xvii–xxxii. All further references to *Fable* are from this edition.

2. Bernard Mandeville, *A Treatise of the Hypochondriack and Hysterick Passions* (London, 1711), pp. 120–21. All further references to *Treatise* are from this edition.

3. *Ibid.*, p. 40.

4. *Treatise, Loc. cit.*

5. *Treatise* (1730), p. xiii, as quoted by Kaye in *Fable*, I, xix–xx.

6. Bernard Mandeville, *The Virgin Unmask'd* (London, 1709), pp. 137–39, 164. All further references to *Virgin Unmask'd* are from this edition.

7. *Ibid.*, p. 171.

8. A year earlier Mandeville had contributed a brief Latin dedicatory poem, signed "B. Mandeville, M.D.," to the medical treatise, *Tutus Cantharidum in Medicina Usus Internus* (London, 1703), by his older fellow-countryman and physician, Joannes Groeneveldt. See H. Gordon Ward, "An Unnoted Poem by Mandeville," *Review of English Studies*, VII (1931), 73–76.

9. See *Virgin Unmask'd*, p. v; and *Treatise*, pp. xii–xiii.

10. In Bernard Mandeville, *A Letter to Dion* (1732), intro. by Jacob Viner, Augustan Reprint Society Publication 41 (Los Angeles, 1952), p. 5, Mandeville remarks: "I have been at Church my self, when the Book in Question has been preach'd against with great Warmth by a worthy Divine, who own'd that he had never seen it." All further references to *Letter to Dion* are from this edition.

11. *Fable*, I, p. cxvi.

12. In listing Mandeville's publications I have mentioned only those whose authenticity is generally accepted. For a list of doubtful works sometimes attributed to Mandeville, see *Fable*, I, xxxi–xxxii and F.B. Kaye, "The Writings of Bernard Mandeville: A Bibliographical Survey," *Journal of English and Germanic Philology*, XX (1921), 419–67. More recently, several other dubious additions to the Mandeville canon have been suggested by Paul B. Anderson and rebutted by Gordon A. Vichert. See Paul Bunyan Anderson, "Bernard Mandeville," *Times Literary Supplement* (November 28, 1936), p. 996; "Splendor Out of Scandal: The Lucinda-Artesia Papers in *The Female Tatler*," *Philological Quarterly*, XV (1936), 286–300; "Cato's Obscure Counterpart in *The British Journal*, 1722–25," *Studies in Philology*,

XXXIV (1937), 412–28; "Bernard Mandeville on Gin," *Publication of the Modern Language Association,* LIV (1939), 775–84. For the rebuttal, see Gordon S. Vichert, "Some Recent Mandeville Attributions," *Philological Quarterly,* XLV (1966), 459–63.

13. As quoted in *Fable,* I, xxv.

14. *Treatise,* p. 52.

15. *Ibid.,* p. 62.

16. *Ibid.,* pp. 153–54.

17. *Fable,* I, 291.

18. Sir John Hawkins, *The Life of Samuel Johnson* (London, 1787), p. 263n.

19. As quoted in *Fable,* I, xxvii.

20. Benjamin Franklin, *Autobiography* (New Haven, 1964), p. 97.

21. *Fable,* I, facing xx.

Chapter Two

1. Bernard Mandeville, *Some Fables After the Easie and Familiar Method of Monsieur de la Fontaine* (London, 1703), pp. iii–v.

2. Bernard Mandeville, *Typhon: Or, the Wars Between the Gods and Giants* (London, 1704), p. v. All line references to *Typhon* are from this edition.

3. *Ibid.,* pp. v–vi.

4. *Fable,* I, 5.

5. Bernard Mandeville, *Aesop Dress'd: Or, a Collection of Fables Writ in Familiar Verse* (London, 1704), intro. by John S. Shea, Augustan Reprint Society Publication 120 (Los Angeles, 1966), p. 41, ll. 1–2. All line references to the fables are from this edition.

6. *Fable,* I, 37n. Kaye notes that the proportion of feminine endings in Mandeville's verse runs as high as 35 percent *(Typhon)* and as low as 7 percent *(Grumbling Hive).*

7. Samuel T. Coleridge, *Coleridge's Miscellaneous Criticism,* ed. by Thomas M. Raysor (Cambridge, Mass., 1936), p. 420.

8. *Treatise,* p. 94.

9. *Virgin Unmask'd,* pp. 171–72.

10. *Aesop Dress'd,* p. ii.

11. John S. Shea, in his introduction to *Aesop Dress'd,* remarks that "Mandeville seems to have been in this work chiefly a translator of La Fontaine" (iii). Shea ascribes the major differences between the two to Mandeville's incapacity, though noting that "some of the . . . changes may be partially justified on the grounds that through them Mandeville was deliberately trying to alter the tone of the poem, to give it an earthiness of spirit congruent with his temperament" (viii).

12. Jean de la Fontaine, *Oeuvre de Jean de la Fontaine,* ed. by

Henri Régnier, 11 vols. (Paris, 1883–1897), I, 13. All line references to La Fontaine's fables are from this edition.

13. La Fontaine, I, 9.

14. Bernard Mandeville, *An Enquiry into the Causes of the Frequent Executions at Tyburn* (London, 1725), intro. by Malvin R. Zirker, Jr., Augustan Reprint Society Publication 105 (Los Angeles, 1964), p. vi. All further references to *Tyburn* are from this edition.

15. In his *De Brutorum Operationibus* (1689), Mandeville argued that no animals have intelligence. Ironically, one of the examples he cited was that of a bee-hive. Admitting that bees superficially seemed ingenious, Mandeville maintained that it would be absurd to credit them with knowledge of science, crafts, and social philosophy.

16. Sturgis E. Leavitt, "Paul Scarron and English Travesty," *Studies in Philology*, XVI, 1 (1919), 108.

17. Bernard Mandeville, *Wishes to a Godson* (London, 1712), p. 5, ll. 39–40.

18. *Aesop Dress'd*, pp. i–ii.

Chapter Three

1. In 1939 Paul B. Anderson published an article entitled "Bernard Mandeville on Gin," *Publication of the Modern Language Association*, LIV (1939), 775–84, in which he attributed to Mandeville the authorship of *A Dissertation Upon Drunkenness*, whose date Anderson gave as 1708. Had Anderson been correct, this would have been Mandeville's earliest prose work. However, Gordon S. Vichert —"Bernard Mandeville and *A Dissertation Upon Drunkenness*," *Notes and Queries*, XI (August, 1964), 288–92—has shown that neither the attribution nor the date Anderson gives for the tract is valid.

2. In the second edition (1724) Mandeville's name is given in full.

3. *Virgin Unmask'd*, p. 1.

4. *The School of Love containing severall dialogues between Tullia and Octavia* (London, 1707) was an adaptation of Nicolas Chorier's *Satyra Sotadica* (c. 1660). See David Foxon, *Libertine Literature in England 1660–1745* (New York, 1965), p. 42.

5. For useful summaries of the major issues and participants in the feminist debate of the seventeenth and eighteenth centuries, see Rae Blanchard, "Richard Steele and the Status of Women," *Studies in Philology*, XXVI (1929), 325–55 and A. R. Humphreys, "The 'Rights of Woman' in the Age of Reason," *Modern Language Review*, XLI (1946), 256–69.

6. *Fable*, I, 69.

7. Bernard Mandeville, *An Enquiry into the Origin of Honour* (London, 1732), p. 59. All further references to *Origin of Honour* are from this edition.

8. Along with many other writers in the "Fair-Sex" debate, Mary Astell and Daniel Defoe both expressed regret that there were no Protestant equivalents to nunneries where single women could devote their lives to virtuous pursuits. Neither, however, presented this alternative as preferable to marriage but as a useful expedient available to some.

Chapter Four

1. For a discussion of the role of melancholia in eighteenth-century English literature, see Cecil A. Moore, *Backgrounds of English Literature 1700–1760* (Minneapolis, 1953), pp. 179–235; and Margery Bailey, intro. to James Boswell's *The Hypochondriack*, 2 vols. (Stanford, 1928), I, 75–89.

2. *Treatise*, pp. vi–vii.

3. Samuel Johnson, "Apophthegms, etc.," in *Johnsonian Miscellanies*, ed. by G. B. Hill, 2 vols. (New York, 1966), II, 20.

4. Denis Leigh, *The Historical Development of British Psychiatry* (New York, 1961), I, 27.

5. Ilza Veith, *Hysteria: The History of a Disease* (Chicago, 1965), p. 154.

Chapter Five

1. Roland N. Stromberg, *Religious Liberalism in Eighteenth-Century England* (Oxford, 1954), p. 1.

2. Bernard Mandeville, *Free Thoughts on Religion, the Church, and National Happiness* (London, 1720), p. xviii. All further references to *Free Thoughts* are from this edition.

3. Beyond his openly avowed debt to Bayle, Mandeville borrows considerably from an author whose influence he does *not* acknowledge—the Third Earl of Shaftesbury. For all his disapproval of Shaftesburian benevolence, Mandeville shared Shaftesbury's ideas on religious toleration, and in the *Free Thoughts* he takes a good many arguments and even some phraseology from Shaftesbury. See Irwin Primer, "A Bibliographical Note on Bernard Mandeville's 'Free Thoughts,' " *Notes and Queries* (May, 1969), 187–88.

4. These two works by Bayle are those most often used by Mandeville, whose references and paraphrases come not from the French originals, but from the English translations—*Miscellaneous Reflections Occasion'd by the Comet* (1708) and *Historical and Critical Dictionary* (1710). See *Fable*, I, xliii, n. 1; 99, nn. 1 and 2; 167, n. 1; and 215, n. 2.

5. Howard Robinson, *Bayle, the Sceptic* (New York, 1931), p. 260.

6. See *Fable*, II, 102, 313.

7. Kathleen Williams, *Jonathan Swift and the Age of Compromise* (Lawrence, Kans., 1958), p. 62.

8. *Letter to Dion*, p. 31.

9. Thomas R. Edwards, Jr., "Mandeville's Moral Prose," *English Literary History*, XXXI (1964), 210n. Not all critics have agreed that Mandeville's rigorism was basically a pose adopted for tactical purposes. For a further endorsement of the sincerity of Mandeville's asceticism, see M. J. Scott-Taggart, "Mandeville: Cynic or Fool," *Philosophical Quarterly*, XVI (1966), 221–32.

Chapter Six

1. *Fable*, I, 95–96.

2. *Ibid.*, I, 385.

3. *Ibid.*, I, 405–06.

4. J. H. Harder, in "The Authorship of *A Modest Defence of Public Stews* Etc.," *Neophilologus*, XVIII (1933), 200–03, questions F. B. Kaye's ascription of this work to Mandeville. Harder—who was evidently unaware that Kaye had fully and convincingly argued the ascription in "The Writings of Bernard Mandeville" (cited above)—claims that Kaye "gives no motives" for assigning the work to Mandeville. It is Harder's dubious contention that Mandeville, having already signed his name or initials to such presumably scandalous works as *The Virgin Unmask'd* and *Wishes to a Godson*, would not have hesitated to acknowledge the "immoral" *Modest Defence* had it been his.

Harder's own candidate for the tract's authorship is "Lawrence Le Fever," whose name he found assigned to the work in an entry (for which Harder gives no year) in the registry at Stationer's Hall. Since Harder admits that his investigation was "somewhat hasty" and that "Further research in the Lib. Brit. Mus. for more information about this writer has, up to the present, had no results," it is rather hard to accept his case. "Lawrence Le Fever," in any event, sounds suspiciously like another of the punning pseudonyms ("Luke Ogle, Esq." is another) which were attached to the *Modest Defence* in its subsequent editions. For a rebuttal of Harder's article, see R. S. Crane, *Philological Quarterly*, XIII, 2 (April, 1934), 122–23.

5. Bernard Mandeville, *A Modest Defence of Public Stews* (London, 1724), intro. by Richard I. Cook, Augustan Reprint Society Publication 162 (Los Angeles, 1973), p. 69. All further references to *Modest Defence* are from this edition.

6. F. B. Kaye, "The Writings of Bernard Mandeville," p. 456.

7. For an account of the Societies for the Reformation of Manners, see W. E. H. Lecky, *A History of England in the Eighteenth Century*, 8 vols. (New York, 1882), II, 594–96.

8. Jonathan Swift, *The Prose Works of Jonathan Swift*, ed. by Herbert Davis, 14 vols. (Oxford, 1937–1968), II, 57.

9. *Fable*, I, 287–88.

10. Daniel Defoe, *Giving Alms No Charity,* as quoted by Louis A. Landa, "A *Modest Proposal* and Populousness," *Modern Philology,* XL (1942), 163. For a further survey of mercantilist ideas in the early eighteenth century, see also George Wittkowsky, "Swift's *Modest Proposal:* The Biography of an Early Georgian Pamphlet," *Journal of the History of Ideas,* IV (1943), 75–104.

11. Mandeville's suggested prices seem very reasonable when compared with an equivalent price list cited half a century later by the anonymous author of *Nocturnal Revels: or the History of King's Place, and other Modern Nunneries* (London, 1779). In the later (and more specialized) list prices ran as high as fifty guineas. For the list, as well as an informative survey of prostitution in eighteenth-century London, see Fernando Henriques, *Prostitution and Society* (London, 1963), II, 143–91.

12. *Tyburn,* p. i.

13. For a full account of Wild's career, see Gerald Howson, *Thief-Taker General: The Rise and Fall of Jonathan Wild* (New York, 1970).

14. For a description of Sheppard's execution, see Christopher Hibbert, *The Road to Tyburn* (Cleveland and New York, 1957), pp. 210–31.

15. For a discussion of eighteenth-century criminal law and penology, see Vol. One of Leon Radzinowicz's *A History of English Criminal Law* (London, 1948).

16. James Boswell, *Life of Johnson* (London, 1960), p. 1211.

Chapter Seven

1. *Fable,* I, 8.

2. Henry Crabb Robinson, *Diary, Reminiscences, and Correspondence,* ed. by Thomas Sadler, 3 vols. (London, 1869), I, 392.

3. Leslie Stephen, *Essays on Free Thinking and Plainspeaking* (London, 1907), p. 279.

4. *Ibid.,* p. 316.

5. See Bertrand A. Goldgar, "Satires on Man and 'The Dignity of Human Nature,' " *Publication of the Modern Language Association,* LXXX (1965), 535–41.

6. Stephen, *op. cit.,* p. 280.

7. Not all students of Mandeville agree that he is lacking in moral fervor. For a capable argument to the contrary, see Thomas H. Edwards, Jr., "Mandeville's Moral Prose" (cited above).

8. Arthur O. Lovejoy, *Reflections on Human Nature* (Baltimore, 1961), p. 179.

9. *Origin of Honour,* pp. 40–41.

10. See, for example, *Fable,* II, 186–87; 321–22.

11. Sterling Lamprecht, *"The Fable of the Bees," Journal of Philosophy,* XXIII, 21 (October, 1926), 565. See also F. A. Hayek,

"Dr. Bernard Mandeville," *Proceedings of the British Academy*, LII (1966), 125–41.

12. For a history of the charity schools, see M. G. Jones, *The Charity School Movement: A Study of Eighteenth-Century Puritanism in Action* (Hamden, Conn., 1964).

13. Thomas H. Edwards, Jr. *(op cit.,* pp. 201–05) has argued that Mandeville's "Essay on Charity and Charity-Schools" is not to be taken at face value. Citing what he calls the "persistent subliminal irony" of the essay, Edwards suggests that Mandeville's indictment of the charity schools is double-edged in that it also contains an implied condemnation of the inequities upon which society bases its treatment of the poor.

It is certainly true, as Edwards points out, that Mandeville does not try to disguise the injustice of the social arrangements he is advocating: conspicuous by their absence from his essay are such time-honored rationalizations as the claim that social priorities are determined by God or that the lower orders are inherently inferior to their rulers. Far from catering to the complacency of his readers, Mandeville makes every effort to force upon them the recognition that selfishness and expediency are the strongest recommendations for keeping the poor in their place. That there is ample irony here at the expense of ruling class hypocrisy is obvious.

None of this, however, makes Mandeville's position any less brutal, unless we assume (as Edwards evidently does) that Mandeville *disapproves* of the harsh treatment accorded the poor. Most students of Mandeville have failed to detect such disapproval, either in the charity school essay or elsewhere in Mandeville's work. See, for example, *Free Thoughts*, p. 332; *Fable*, I, 119–20, 185–98, 248; and *Tyburn, passim.*

14. Jones, *op cit.,* pp. 4–5.

15. Swift, for example, makes a similar point in Gulliver's description of the admirable educational policies which the Lilliputians have so foolishly allowed to lapse. Under these laws, we learn: "The Cottagers and Labourers keep their Children at home, their Business being only to till and cultivate the Earth; and therefore their Education is of little Consequence to the Publick; but the Old and Diseased among them are supported by Hospitals: For begging is a Trade unknown in this Empire"—*Prose Works* (cited above), IX, 63. See also *Fable*, I, lxx–lxxi.

16. *Free Thoughts*, p. 239.

17. The letters of "Cato," which had been appearing since 1720, were the work of John Trenchard (1622–1723) and Thomas Gordon (d. 1759). Originally published weekly in the *London Journal*, these letters took a strong Whiggish and anti-High Church position. The specific letters which aroused the Grand Jury's ire were those of

March, May, and June, 1723. In these, religious superstition, clerical tyranny, and the charity schools are all denounced. "Cato's" arguments against the latter are similar to Mandeville's, but with a much heavier emphasis on the charity schools as training grounds for Popery and High Church politics.

18. For summaries and a discussion of these and other contemporary answers to Mandeville, see Paul Sakmann, *Bernard de Mandeville und die Bienenfabel-Controverse* (Freiburg, Leipzig, and Tübingen, 1897); also see *Fable*, II, 401–53.

19. Even within the confines of the relatively formal essays that compose most of Part I of the *Fable*, Mandeville, by periodically introducing an imaginary *adversarius*, had sought to approximate the give and take of a dialogue. Thus, in "Remark G," for example, he presents in some detail the objections his argument might elicit from "a sharp-sighted good-humour'd Man" (I, 92); and in "Remark T" he fancies himself "interrupted by an *Epicure*" (I, 233) whose imagined comments are dramatically given. Somewhat analogous are those passages in Part I where Mandeville anticipates with imaginary examples the criticism he expects his book to inspire. See, for example, *Fable*, I, 117, 268–69, and 291–92.

20. Donald Davie, "Berkeley and the Style of Dialogue," *The English Mind: Studies in the English Moralists Presented to Basil Willey*, ed. by Hugh Davies and George Watson (Cambridge, 1964), p. 105. In his remarks Davie misidentifies Horatio as "Antonio."

21. For a discussion of Mandeville's use of Horatio to evade responsibility for unorthodox sentiments, see *Fable*, II, 21, n. 2. Further examples may be found in *Fable*, II, 196–97, 205–07, 218–21, 236–39, and 320–21.

22. See, for example, Berkeley's dismissal of non-Mosaic chronology in *The Works of George Berkeley, Bishop of Cloyne*, ed. by A. A. Luce and T. E. Jessop, 9 vols. (London, 1948–1957), III, 258ff.

23. For a further discussion of Mandeville's ideas on the beginnings of speech, see F. B. Kaye, "Mandeville on the Origin of Language," *Modern Language Notes*, XXXIX (1924), 136–42.

24. In this connection it is interesting to note that during Mandeville's lifetime Parts I and II of the *Fable* were issued independently and by different publishers. It was not until 1733—after Mandeville's death—that both sections appeared together in a two-volume edition. The *Origin of Honour* (with yet another publisher) has not to my knowledge ever been issued together with Parts I and II, though it is obviously intended as a continuation of the latter.

25. *Origin of Honour*, p. 40.

26. *Ibid.*, pp. 81–82.

27. *Ibid.*, p. 240.

Chapter Eight

1. George Berkeley, *The Works of George Berkeley* (cited above), III, 23. All page references to *Alciphron* are from this edition.

2. In keeping with Berkeley's contention that all minute philosophers are fundamentally much the same, Alciphron's Shaftesburianism is eclectic enough to include a number of contradictory Mandevillean tenets—as, for example, the idea that morality and religious systems are the inventions of "skilful rulers." On the whole, however, it is Lysicles who most specifically represents Mandeville's viewpoint, occasionally in the face of polite disagreement from Alciphron.

3. *Fable*, II, 32ff.

4. Viner, intro. to *Letter to Dion*, p. 1.

5. J. C. Maxwell, "Ethics and Politics in Mandeville," *Philosophy*, XXVI (1951), 242, n. 1.

6. In addition to the *Letter to Dion*, Berkeley was answered (mostly on Shaftesbury's behalf) by John Hervey's *Some Remarks on "The Minute Philosopher"* (London, 1732); by letters in the *London Journal* of May 18, 1732 and in the *Daily Post-boy* of September 9, 1732; and by Bishop Peter Browne's *Things Divine and Supernatural* (London, 1733).

7. Maxwell, *loc. cit.*

8. Bernard Mandeville, *Letter to Dion*, ed. by Bonamy Dobrée (Liverpool, 1954), p. vii.

9. *Ibid.*, pp. ix–x.

10. As quoted in *Fable*, I, xxix–xxx, no. 6.

11. *Ibid.*, II, 418ff.

12. *Ibid.*, I, cxvii, n. 5.

13. *Ibid.*, I, cxviii.

14. Edwards, *op. cit.*, p. 212.

Selected Bibliography

PRIMARY SOURCES

There is no collected edition of Mandeville's works. For those individual works not reprinted in modern times, I have cited the first edition.

Aesop Dress'd: Or, a Collection of Fables Writ in Familiar Verse (1704). Intro. by John S. Shea. Augustan Reprint Society Publication Number 120. Los Angeles: Clark Library, 1966.

Typhon: Or, the Wars Between the Gods and Giants: A Burlesque Poem in Imitation of the Comical Mons. Scarron. London: J. Pero and S. Illidge, 1704.

The Virgin Unmask'd: Or, Female Dialogues Betwixt an Elderly Maiden Lady, and Her Niece. London: J. Morphew and J. Woodward, 1709.

A Treatise of the Hypochondriack and Hysterick Passions. London: Dryden Leach and W. Taylor, 1711. A somewhat altered version was issued in 1730 under the title *A Treatise of the Hypochondriack and Hysterick Diseases.*

Wishes to a Godson, with Other Miscellany Poems. London: J. Baker, 1712.

The Fable of the Bees: Or, Private Vices, Publick Benefits. 2 vols. Ed. by F. B. Kaye. Oxford: Clarendon Press, 1924 (reissued 1957). This definitive edition (based on the 1732 Part I and the 1729 Part II) is an invaluable document for the study of Mandeville. Kaye's introduction, notes, and appendixes provide the basis from which most subsequent Mandeville scholarship has proceeded.

The Fable of the Bees: Or, Private Vices, Publick Benefits. Ed. by Irwin Primer. New York: Capricorn Books, 1962. Useful abridgement.

The Fable of the Bees: Or, Private Vices, Publick Benefits. Ed. by Phillip Harth. London: Penguin Books, 1970. An edition, based on modern editing principles, of the *Fable,* Part I.

Free Thoughts on Religion, the Church, and National Happiness. London: T. Jauncy and J. Roberts, 1720.

A Modest Defence of Publick Stews, or, an Essay upon Whoring, As It Is Now Practis'd in These Kingdoms (1724). Intro. by Richard I. Cook. Augustan Reprint Society Publication Number 162. Los Angeles: Clark Library, 1973.

An Enquiry into the Causes of the Frequent Executions at Tyburn

(1725). Intro. by Malvin R. Zirker, Jr. Augustan Reprint Society Publication Number 105. Los Angeles: Clark Library, 1964.

An Enquiry into the Causes of the Frequent Executions at Tyburn (1725). Facsimile of the first edition. Menston: Scolar Press, 1971.

An Enquiry into the Origin of Honour, and the Usefulness of Christianity in War (1732). Facsimile of the first edition. Intro. by M. M. Goldsmith. London: Cass & Co., 1971.

A Letter to Dion, Occasion'd by His Book Call'd Alciphron (1732). Intro. by Jacob Viner. Augustan Reprint Society Publication Number 41. Los Angeles: Clark Library, 1953. Viner's introduction has been reprinted in *The Long View and the Short*, Glencoe, Illinois: Free Press, 1958.

A Letter to Dion, Occasion'd by His Book Call'd Alciphron (1732). Intro. by Bonamy Dobrée. Liverpool: University Press of Liverpool, 1954.

SECONDARY SOURCES

In F. B. Kaye's edition of *The Fable of the Bees* (II, 418–53—cited above), a detailed list of references to Mandeville and his works covers the years 1716 to 1923.

ALPERS, PAUL J. "Pope's *To Bathurst* and the Mandevillean State," *English Literary History*, XXV (1958), 23–42. Reprinted in Maynard Mack, ed., *Essential Articles for the Study of Alexander Pope*. Hamden, Conn.: Archon Books, 1964. Contends that Pope's poem, which has been called Mandevillean in outlook, is actually in "fundamental opposition to Mandeville."

ANDERSON, PAUL B. "Splendor Out of Scandal: The Lucinda-Artesia Papers in *The Female Tatler*," *Philological Quarterly*, XV (1936), 286–300. Attributes these essays to Mandeville. See Gordon S. Vichert (below).

———. "Bernard Mandeville," *Times Literary Supplement*, November 28, 1936, p. 996. Attributes a series of letters in *The Weekly Journal* to Mandeville. See Gordon S. Vichert (below).

———. "Innocence and Artifice: or, Mrs. Centlivre and *The Female Tatler*," *Philological Quarterly*, XVI (1937), 358–75. Suggests that Mandeville collaborated with Susannah Centlivre in *The Female Tatler*. See Gordon S. Vichert (below).

———. "Cato's Obscure Counterpart in *The British Journal*, 1722–25," *Studies in Philology*, XXXIV (1937), 412–28. Detects Mandeville's hand in the letters of "Diogenes," "Criton," and "Philanthropos." See Gordon S. Vichert (below).

———. "Bernard Mandeville on Gin," *Publication of the Modern Language Association*, LIV (1939), 775–84. Attributes *A Disser-*

tation on Drunkenness (1727) to Mandeville. See Gordon S. Vichert (below).

BLUET, GEORGE (also spelled "BLEWITT" and "BLUETT"). *An Enquiry Whether a General Practice of Virtue Tends to the Wealth or Poverty, Benefit or Disadvantage of a People?* London: W. Wilkin, 1725. One of the ablest of the early criticisms of Mandeville's economic theory.

CHIASSON, ELIAS J. "Bernard Mandeville: A Reappraisal," *Philological Quarterly,* XLIX, 4 (October, 1970), 489–519. An essay arguing that the main elements of Mandeville's philosophy place him not, as usually thought, in the skeptical tradition of Hobbes, but rather in the Christian humanist tradition of Hooker.

CRANE, R. S. Review of J. H. Harder's "The Authorship of *A Modest Defence of Publick Stews"* (see below), *Philological Quaterly,* XIII, 2 (April, 1934), 122–23. Rejects the argument of Harder that the work is not Mandeville's.

DECKELMANN, WILHELM. *Untersuchung zur Bienenfabel Mandevilles und zu Ihrer Enstehungsgeschichte in Hinblick auf die Bienenfabelthese.* Hamburg: Friederischen, de Guyter & Co., 1933. Discussion of the influences on Mandeville's thought.

DOBRÉE, BONAMY. *Variety of Ways.* Oxford: Clarendon Press, 1932. Chapter VI (100–18) briefly treats of the background, style, and influence of *The Fable of the Bees.*

EDWARDS, THOMAS R. "Mandeville's Moral Prose," *English Literary History,* XXXI (1964), 195–212. Edwards vigorously argues that the intensity, seriousness, and complexity of Mandeville's moral vision has been underrated by previous critics. He concludes that Mandeville's prose, which was informed by that vision, "has an enduring claim as literature of a high order indeed."

GOLDGAR, BERTRAND A. "Satires on Man and the 'Dignity of Human Nature,'" *Publication of the Modern Language Association,* LXXX (1965), 535–41. Discusses the contemporary response to those satirists—Swift, Gay, and Mandeville—who took a dark view of human nature.

HARDER, J. H. "The Authorship of *A Modest Defence of Public* [Sic] *Stews* Etc.," *Neophilologus,* XVIII (1933), 200–03. Argues that the work is not Mandeville's, but "Lawrence Le Fever's." See Crane (cited above).

HARTH, PHILLIP. "The Satiric Purpose of *The Fable of the Bees,*" *Eighteenth-Century Studies,* II (1969), 321–40. Contends that Mandeville's critics (particularly Kaye) have failed to distinguish how Mandeville's satiric emphases and targets shifted as the *Fable* grew by accretion over three decades.

HAYEK, F. A. "Dr. Bernard Mandeville," *Proceedings of the British Academy,* LII (1966), 125–41. Discusses Mandeville's contributions to psychological and evolutionary theory.

HIND, GEORGE. "Mandeville's *Fable of the Bees* as Menippean Satire," *Genre*, I (1968), 307–15.

JONES, HARRY L. "Holberg on Mandeville's *Fable of the Bees*," *College Language Association Journal*, IV (1960), 116–25.

KAYE, F. B. "The Writings of Bernard Mandeville: A Bibliographical Survey," *Journal of English and Germanic Philology*, XX (1921), 419–67. A listing (with description and explanatory discussion) of works demonstrably by Mandeville, others possibly by him, and still others erroneoulsy attributed to him. This listing is superceded by that in Kaye's edition of *The Fable of the Bees* (cited above), but is valuable for its discussions.

————. "The Influence of Bernard Mandeville," *Studies in Philology*, XIX (1922), 83–108. Superceded by Kaye's introduction to his edition of *The Fable of the Bees* (cited above).

————. "Mandeville on the Origin of Language," *Modern Language Notes*, XXXIX (1924), 136–42.

————. "The Mandeville Canon: A Supplement," *Notes & Queries*, May 3, 1924, 317–21. Discusses and rejects a series of attributions to Mandeville.

LAMPRECHT, STERLING P. "*The Fable of the Bees*," *Journal of Philosophy*, XXIII, 21 (October, 1926), 561–79. Perceptive appreciation of Mandeville as a moral theorist.

LAW, WILLIAM. *Remarks Upon a Late Book Entituled, The Fable of the Bees*. London: W. and J. Innys, 1724. Perhaps the best of the contemporary works in opposition to the *Fable*.

MAXWELL, J. C. "Ethics and Politics in Mandeville," *Philosophy*, XXVI (1951), 242–52. Asserts Mandeville's importance as a pioneer in the field of the relation of ethics to politics.

MINER, EARL R. "Dr. Johnson, Mandeville, and 'Publick Benefits,'" *Huntington Library Quarterly*, XXI (1958), 159–66. Stresses Johnson's disagreement with Mandeville's doctrines.

NOXON, JAMES. "Dr. Mandeville: 'A Thinking Man,'" *The Varied Pattern: Studies in the 18th Century*. Ed. Peter Hughes and David Williams. Toronto, 1971, pp. 233–52. Noxon discusses Mandeville's affinities with Hobbes and maintains that Mandeville (though his purposes are often ambiguous) intends his work essentially as an indictment of society's practice of self-indulgence while preaching self-denial.

PLAMENATZ, JOHN. *The English Utilitarians*. Oxford: Blackwell, 1966. Argues Mandeville cannot be considered an exponent of *laissez-faire* economics.

PREU, JAMES. "Private Vices—Public Benefits," *English Journal*, LII (1963), 653–58, 692. General outline of Mandeville's ideas.

PRICE, MARTIN. *To the Palace of Wisdom: Studies in Order and Energy from Dryden to Blake*. New York: Doubleday, 1964. Chapter IV ("Mandeville: Order as Art") contains an excellent account of Mandeville's moral thought and the nature of his literary achievement.

PRIMER, IRWIN. "A Bibliographical Note on Bernard Mandeville's 'Free Thoughts,'" *Notes and Queries*, CCXIV (May, 1969), 187–88. Shows that much of the enlarged second edition (1729) of the *Free Thoughts on Religion* is borrowed verbatim from Bayle and Shaftesbury with a view toward increasing the book's influence in furthering Whig principles.

ROGERS, A. K. "The Ethics of Mandeville," *International Journal of Ethics*, XXXVI (1925), 1–17. Lucidly analyzes Mandeville as "a moral realist, who is not so much engaged in setting forth a theory of virtue as he is exposing the pretensions to virtue in the human animal."

ROSENBERG, NATHAN. "Mandeville and Laissez-Faire," *Journal of the History of Ideas*, XXIV (1963), 183–96. Explores Mandeville's attitudes toward the economic doctrines of *laissez-faire* and mercantilism.

SAKMANN, PAUL. *Bernard de Mandeville und die Bienenfabel-Controverse*. Freiburg, Leipzig, and Tübingen: J. C. B. Mohr, 1897. Most comprehensive study of the controversy inspired by *The Fable of the Bees*.

SCHATZ, ALBERT. *L'Individualisme Economique et Social*. Paris: Colin, 1907. Discusses Mandeville as an anticipator of many of Adam Smith's economic doctrines. For a contrary view, see Jacob Viner's introduction to *The Letter to Dion* and John Palamenatz's book (both cited above).

SCOTT-TAGGART, M. J. "Mandeville: Cynic or Fool," *Philosophical Quarterly*, XVI (1966), 221–32. Disagrees with the traditional view that Mandeville, in *The Fable of the Bees*, offers a *reductio ad absurdum* of rigorist morality. Scott-Taggart contends that Mandeville's position is logical and tenable in the very terms in which it is presented, and he concludes that "Mandeville, beneath his irony, was a serious moralist who deserves to be taken seriously...."

SMITH, LEROY W. "Fielding and Mandeville: The 'War Against Virtue,'" *Criticism*, III (1961), 75–85. Contends that Fielding, despite his expressed benevolence, shows a considerable affinity to Mandeville's skeptical view of human nature and society.

STEPHEN, SIR LESLIE. *Essays on Freethinking and Plainspeaking*. London: Smith, Elder and Co., 1907. Chapter VII—"Mandeville's *Fable of the Bees*"—is a valuable analysis, albeit one which exaggerates Mandeville's "crudity."

VICHERT, GORDON S. "Bernard Mandeville and *A Dissertation Upon Drunkenness*," *Notes and Queries*, Second Series, XI (August, 1964), 288–92. Refutes P. B. Anderson's attribution (cited above) of this work to Mandeville.

————. "Some Recent Mandeville Attributions," *Philological Quarterly*, XLV (1966), 459–63. Rejects P. B. Anderson's ascriptions to Mandeville (cited above), with the exception of the Lucinda-Artesia papers in *The Female Tatler*.

WARD, H. GORDON. "An Unnoted Poem by Mandeville," *Review of English Studies*, VII (1931), 73–76. Notes Latin verses (signed "B. Mandeville, M.D.") prefixed to a medical treatise of 1703 by J. Groeneveldt.

WHATELY, RICHARD. *Introductory Lectures on Political Economy: Being Part of a Course Delivered in Easter Term, 1831.* London: B. Fellowes, 1832. Lecture II includes an acute analysis of Mandeville's thought.

WILDE, NORMAN. "Mandeville's Place in English Thought," *Mind: A Quarterly Review of Psychology and Philosophy*, New Series, VII (1898), 219–32. Mandeville's role as an opponent of Shaftesbury.

YOUNG, JAMES D. "Mandeville: A Popularizer of Hobbes," *Modern Language Notes*, LXXIV (1959), 10–13. Claims that Mandeville departs from Hobbes in the application of ethics in politics.

Index